What People Are Saying About *StormProof* and *StormProof*...

As a youth, a wise man told me that when choosing companions for life's journey, I should look for those fellow "soldiers" who had dented armor. Those with shiny and pristine armor would be of little help when it came to navigating life's battles. Carol McLeod is one of those valiant warriors with dented, scratched, and scuffed armor. If you are seeking advice on how to survive the storms of life, you've found someone who knows firsthand what it means to not just survive them, but also to exit them better in all the ways that really matter.

—*Chris Busch*
CEO and President, LightQuest Media. Inc.

StormProof: Weathering Life's Tough Times might just be Carol McLeod's best work yet. Why? Because this woman of God knows a thing or two about storms, having thrived in the midst of some of the worst of life's tempests. I believe this book was birthed from a place of authenticity and revelation about biblical storms. A must-read for every believer!

—*Johnie Hampton*
CEO and President, Hampton Creative

Stormproof is a great reminder of God's faithfulness through every life circumstance we encounter. As your spiritual meteorologist, Carol McLeod will give you a closer look at the eye of biblical storms so you can learn how to persevere through life's downpours and be ignited with hope to see the rainbow at the end of them.

—*Keri Cardinale*
Worship leader, author, and radio host

Carol McLeod reveals a triple-layered, foolproof way to not only survive life's storms, but also prevail and pioneer the way for others into places and spaces of stability and destiny: she highlights powerful biblical stories, testifies of her own navigation in troubled waters, and offers appropriate challenges to the reader to be anchored in the face of his or her own circumstantial cyclones. Whether you have just emerged from a storm or are still in the middle of one, *StormProof* is a must to help you safely navigate through the inevitable, sometimes violent, storms of life. There is always a way through, no matter what. Carol clearly defines that way.

—*Christy Christopher*
Author and speaker
National Prayer Coordinator, Carol McLeod Ministries

We all have experienced storms in our lives. Maybe you are in the eye of one right now, hunkered down and wondering how you will survive. Well, as usual, we can count on Carol McLeod to show us that there is a way out. We don't have to struggle through the waters alone, and the choices we make can keep us *StormProof*!

—*Maggie John*
Host, *100 Huntley Street* television program

Carol McLeod weaves her wealth of wisdom and disarming compassion throughout this must-have survival guide for weathering life's storms. She offers rich insights and critical principles from stories in Scripture that both challenge and comfort us to trust in the God who calms our storms.

—*Angela Donadio*
Author, *Finding Joy When Life Is Out of Focus:*
Philippians—A Study for Joy-Thirsty Women

Most of us have been through a major life storm—or soon will be and just don't know it yet. In *Stormproof*, Carol McLeod gives you more than a life preserver; she shows you how to exercise the kind of faith to help you metaphorically walk on water—and also rise above the waves and beyond the clouds. There's no guarantee you will avoid the wind and whitecaps, but you can grow wiser and stronger as you weather whatever life throws your way.

—*Anita Agers-Brooks*
Inspirational business/life coach and international speaker
Award-winning author, *Getting Through What You Can't Get Over* and
*Exceedingly: Spiritual Strategies for Living on Purpose, with Purpose, and for
an Abundant Purpose*
Host, *Tending Your Dreams* podcast

Stormproof: Weathering Life's Tough Times by Carol McLeod is a unique look at the storms described in the Bible in order to find comfort and encouragement as we face our own difficult days. Carol offers an exploration of different storms and their causes, various ways to respond to them, and how all of this can be applied to our lives in a helpful way. There are penetrating questions encouraging us to cry out to God and allow the Comforter to minister to our hurting souls in times of trouble. This book delivers a guide to become "more captivated by the Savior than by the storm." Hope and healing await all who read this compelling book.

—*Kim Erickson*
Author, *His Last Words* and *Sorrow & Survival: A Mother's Guide*
(September 2019)

Stormproof is another beautiful reminder of God's unending faithfulness to us, no matter what is going on around us. Carol examines the storms in the Bible and makes practical application to our lives. She brings the Word to life, enabling us to see that help is only a prayer away.

—*Donna Russo*
Executive Director and CFO, Kingdom Bound Ministries

I picked up Carol McLeod's book *StormProof* hours after a storm erupted in my life. Thankfully, God had been preparing me for it, but Carol's sound teaching and convincing faith in God's Word helped me stay grounded with wisdom and reminded me to set anchors of hope in His promises. If not for the comfort of God's presence through the well-timed messages in this book, I could easily have felt flattened by the winds battering at my heart! Read this book if you are weary of fearing inevitable storms in your life. Read it if you not only want to survive your storms, but also grow stronger because of them. Read this book if you need assurance of God's comfort in the midst of this world's chaos!

—*Heather DeJesus Yates*
Attorney, speaker, blogger, and author, *All the Wild Pearls: A Guide for Passing Down Redemptive Stories*

Like most people, I don't enjoy storms, but after reading Carol McLeod's book *Stormproof: Weathering Life's Tough Times*, I am better equipped to weather any turbulence that interrupts the tranquility of my life. Resonating off each page is the victorious voice of my friend Carol, head held high, facing directly into any adverse winds, full of faith and hope. Her years of treasure hunting in the Word of God have equipped her to write this book, but its real power lies in the fact that she hasn't simply studied hurricanes from the security of a safe harbor but has also experienced them as a sailor navigating the storms of life, with Jesus Christ Himself co-piloting her boat. This book will empower you to triumph in tough times.

—*Faith Blatchford*
Author, *Winning the Battle for the Night: God's Plan for Sleep, Dreams and Revelation*
www.faithblatchford.com

Funny, thought-provoking, and filled with the love of Jesus, *StormProof* is another Carol McLeod masterpiece that will lead the reader into the heart of God. Carol takes us on a journey through Scripture, uncovering hidden nuances and truth gems she discovered only through her intimate relationship with the Scripture's Author. *Stormproof* is a must-read as we navigate the storms of life. It will help us come through each storm we encounter wiser, stronger, and more in love with Jesus.

—Pastor Melissa G. Bolden
MBoldenMinistry
Author, teacher, and international speaker

The storms of life *will* come, but with this book from Carol McLeod, we're equipped to face the tempest. Using a foundation of solid biblical teaching and adding her own insight and personal experiences, McLeod has presented us with a wonderful gift. *StormProof* is a volume I'll return to again and again.

—Edie Melson
Speaker and author, *Soul Care When You're Weary* and *Maiden of Iron*
Social Media Director, *Southern Writers* magazine
Author, *The Write Conversation* blog

It would be difficult for me to recommend anyone else more qualified by their life experiences than Carol McLeod to tell such biblical stories as Paul's harrowing tale of being caught in a violent storm at sea. Indeed, a person doesn't have much more to share with someone else than their own story. Carol's story is one of perils, faith, faithfulness, and triumphs. The ship of her life should have been dashed on the rocks many times, but she clearly has her soul anchored to the hope that never fails. In *StormProof: Weathering Life's Tough Times*, you will learn how your own soul can be bonded securely to Christ in the midst of any storm.

—Tim Cameron
Speaker and author, *The Forty-Day Word Fast* and *40 Days Through the Prayers of Jesus*

When life's winds and waves overwhelm us, we ask: Is there a God? Does He love me? Am I significant in the universe? Having experienced both heartbreaking challenges and God's life-giving presence, author Carol McLeod gently connects your heart to God's grace-filled guidance with the assurance, *"Everyone who trusts in him will never be put to shame"* (Romans 10:11 NIV84).

—*PeggySue Wells*
Best-selling author of twenty-eight books, including *Bonding with Your Child Through Boundaries* (with June Hunt), *Rediscovering Your Happily Ever After*, and *Homeless for the Holidays* (with Marsha J. Wright)

In life, storms will come—of this we can be certain. After the devastation of Hurricane Andrew, the state of Florida changed its building codes. In *StormProof*, Carol McLeod opens the biblical code book and wisely encourages us to build a strong spiritual foundation by embracing and acting upon God's Word. Be encouraged and full of hope—be *StormProof*.

—*Suzanne Brooks Kuhn*
Author, speaker, and entrepreneur
Founder, SuzyQ
CEO and Chief Creative Officer, Brookstone Creative Group

Life's storms are unexpected and leave us with a choice: to become bitter or better. Carol McLeod's personal and practical book *StormProof* gives you the tools to prepare for any looming tempests you may face and to anchor your feet in faith so that you remain steady and confident in the midst of them. She provides simple steps to come through these storms victoriously—equipped and empowered as never before. This book is a raincoat of truth to don immediately in this season of your life or tuck away for the next rainfall, but every Christian needs it for protection from the storms of life!

—*Erica Wiggenhorn*
Speaker and author, An Unexplainable Life Bible study series and The Unexplainable Church Bible study series

We live in a fallen, broken world, and at some point, we will all be touched by one of life's storms. But that doesn't have to mean we will get swept up and away, to live defeated and discouraged. On the contrary, in *StormProof*, Carol McLeod lovingly and wisely points us to the hope that exists in every life storm, encouraging us, guiding us, and offering us wisdom for how to keep our eyes on that hope—on Jesus. This book is a great reminder that we serve an all-powerful God, One who effortlessly walks on top of those stormy waves and keeps us from sinking beneath them. If you're facing storms in life, I highly recommend this book. If you're not currently facing any storms, I highly recommend this book—because it will help you prepare for when they do come.

—Lynette Eason
Award-winning, best-selling author, the Blue Justice series

Prepare to be "blown away" by Carol McLeod's new book, *StormProof*. When life tries to sweep you off course, this engaging book will help you discover unexpected comfort, joy, and determination. You will see God's goodness in the midst of your storm and His faithfulness in unwelcome conditions. Wow, don't we all need that!

—John Mason
Best-selling author of numerous books,
including *An Enemy Called Average*

In *StormProof: Weathering Life's Tough Times*, Carol McLeod helps us triumphantly navigate the storms in life as she takes us on a voyage across the unpredictable oceans we often traverse. You will be encouraged and uplifted as Carol transparently shares her own journey and helps us to identify some of the purposes of our storms while teaching us how to respond to them. This new book by Carol is truly a must-read for anyone who has felt battered by life's storms.

—Donna Sparks
Author, *Beauty from Ashes: My Story of Grace*

STORM

Proof

Weathering Life's Tough Times

CAROL McLEOD

STORM
Proof

Weathering Life's Tough Times

W

WHITAKER
HOUSE

StormProof:
Weathering Life's Tough Times

Carol Burton McLeod
carol@carolmcleodministries.com
www.carolmcleodministries.com
Carol McLeod Ministries
PO Box 1274
Orchard Park, NY 14127
855-569-5433

ISBN: 978-1-64123-221-0 • eBook ISBN: 978-1-64123-222-7
Printed in the United States of America
© 2019 by Carol Burton McLeod

Whitaker House
1030 Hunt Valley Circle
New Kensington, PA 15068
www.whitakerhouse.com

Library of Congress Cataloging-in-Publication Data (Pending)

1 2 3 4 5 6 7 8 9 10 11 ⨆⨆ 26 25 24 23 22 21 20 19

This book is lovingly and sincerely dedicated to:

Diane Marie Eick Phelps,

a lifetime friend and a woman who has survived the
worst of life's storms.

You have danced in the sunshine...been drenched by
circumstantial downpours...been threatened by windy
situations...and been attacked by the blinding blizzard
of events.

But through it all, you have been faithful.

You have been a warrior.

You have been a worshipper.

You have kept your eyes on Jesus.

You have been *StormProof.*

You haven't just weathered the tough times in life...you have
rejoiced through them!

There is no one I would rather share an umbrella with than
you,
my friend.

Contents

Part Three: *An Epic Saga*

Part Four: *Mea Culpa!*

Part Five: *The Final Answer to All of Your Storm Questions*

Part Six: *Speak to the Storm*

Part Seven: *The Aftermath*

Foreword

As I write this foreword, our nation is reeling from the destruction of Hurricane Michael, which slammed into the Florida Panhandle with a vengeance in October 2018. News reports are filled with stories of rescuers still searching the rubble for survivors, of houses that were destroyed, and of trees that were leveled. People from the hardest-hit areas wonder if they will ever recover.

Similarly, various personal storms in our lives often leave us devastated and wondering if we'll ever be able to bounce back. Carol McLeod knows this place of devastation and depression. But when I think of who Carol is, two words come to mind: *steady* and *strong*. She's been through some of the toughest personal storms an individual can endure—losing babies, battling cancer, facing financial difficulty, and a host of other trials. Most of us would have collapsed under such hardship and quite possibly ditched our faith. Yet, through every storm, Carol has remained steady and strong.

Over the years, as I have watched her life, Carol has reminded me of the person described by the Old Testament prophet Jeremiah:

*But blessed is the one who trusts in the L*ORD*, whose confidence is in him. They will be like a tree planted by the water that sends out its roots by the stream. It does not fear when heat comes; its leaves are always green. It has no worries in a year of drought and never fails to bear fruit.* —Jeremiah 17:7–8 NIV

How does Carol remain steady and strong?

The answer to that question lies in the book you're about to read. Carol has rooted herself deeply in God's Word and spent much time in His presence praising Him. Praise was her mantra even on the most difficult days. As a result, her roots have held her steady and strong—not only during seasons of drought, but also when the hurricane and tornado winds have blown.

Friend, the truth is that storms will blow (and probably already have blown) into your life as well. The question is, how firm will you remain? Will your roots hold you steady? As you read this profound book, you will not find pious platitudes or pithy solutions. What you will find are truths that are rooted deeply in God's Word and will stand the storms of time.

Before you begin reading, I want to suggest that you pray, "Lord Jesus, help me to learn from Carol how to have my roots sink firmly into Your Word. Show me what it looks like to stormproof my life so that I might remain steady and strong throughout every gale. Use this book in a profound way in my life, I pray!"

—*Becky Harling*
Author, *The 30-Day Praise Challenge, How to Listen so People Will Talk,*
and *Who Do You Say That I A*M?

Introduction:
The Shelter of God's Presence

What storm has blown into your life lately? Are you—or is someone you love—suffering from the trauma of plans that have been washed away, relationships that have been uprooted, or security that has been devastated?

Rather than being destroyed by this tempest, what if you allowed the disturbance to increase your capacity for rapid growth and fulfilling your destiny in God? Instead of suffering for years after the comprehensive wreckage that a vicious whirlwind in life inflicts, what if you allowed that same storm to clear out unnecessary undergrowth, weeds, and blockages in your life?

The sobering truth is that no storm leaves you the way it found you. You will either grow stronger due to lessons learned in the storm or you will become weaker due to the ferocious winds you have encountered. After digging deeply into the Word of God, I believe that there is a way—a triumphant way—to encounter the fierce gales of life and then exit those tempests with strength, resilience, and joy. There is a definitive way to walk through the most devastating of circumstances and emerge with grace and hope, empowered for the future. There is a way to be *StormProof*!

I am a storm survivor. More than that, I am a storm overcomer—having contended with depression, infertility, and cancer and yet having emerged stronger in faith and deeper in my love for God. Everyone encounters storms while living this side of heaven's placid shores. They are a common occurrence in every season of our lives. No one is immune to situational squalls, relational disturbances, or circumstantial blizzards. However, for a believer in Christ, the damage such storms cause can be contained, depending on how we navigate their tumultuous waves.

There are promises in the Bible that will enable you to find protection in the safest and most secure shelter in all of eternity. That place is in God's presence, and His presence alone. I believe with my whole heart that God has good plans for you and that His sweet presence offers peaceful restitution for your life on the "after" side of the storm. Knowing we have been promised His presence, we then must ask ourselves: "What should a believer do during a stormy season in life?" "Is it really possible to outlast an unremitting storm with determination and joy?"

Storms in the Bible

To answer these questions, *StormProof* takes a fascinating and focused look at storms from a scriptural perspective. Together, we will go storm-chasing through the pages of the greatest Book ever written, observing various biblical tempests and how they may have impacted those who were caught up in them.

You will step out of the boat to walk the waves with Peter, knowing that Jesus always comes to be with you in the midst of your storms; you will be rocked aboard a wind-driven ship with the apostle Paul, in danger of being smashed against the rocks, but be preserved by God's power; you will watch the gathering storm clouds with Noah, holding on to faith in God's purposes. You will also experience Jonah's self-inflicted tempest while affirming God's unconditional love, sit in silence with Job and ponder his questions about the greatest storm of *testing*, and huddle with the disciples as their boat is swamped by surging waves—only to hear Jesus's eternal words, "Peace, be still." You will also hear about storms of harsh circumstances that others from recent history have encountered and overcome.

As I studied these storms, I realized that the lessons the biblical figures learned from the horrific blasts they experienced—either through their righteous responses or their seriously mistaken reactions—had teaching potential for those of us who are serving Christ in the twenty-first century. The storms recorded in the Bible are not just ancient stories; they hold practical application for storm-weary travelers today.

For whatever was written in earlier times was written for our instruction, so that through perseverance and the encouragement of the Scriptures we might have hope. —Romans 15:4

In *StormProof*, we will gaze from the grandstand of history, exiting each storm with a heavenly perspective concerning the necessary preparation for, the inherent power of, and the remaining purpose of, that storm. After observing the tempests that are chronicled in the Bible, you will find both wise solutions and everyday answers for how to always remain in a place of safety and protection during difficulties. Yet even beyond safety and protection, you will see that the Bible promises a vibrant *comeback* for any child of the King who encounters an unexpected whirlwind.

I believe that the Holy Spirit placed each storm story in the Bible so we could learn to persevere, be encouraged, and have hope. What an exciting possibility!

Storm Queries and Answers

Still, it is often hard for many people to reconcile the fact that God *allows* such storms in our lives. Even a Christian of bold faith might be tempted to ask a question or two when tornadic conditions are spotted on the horizon of life. Many believers have been known to query, "God! *Where are You* in this storm?" Others may even have the sincere audacity to interrogate God with this accusatory cross-examination: "God, why did *You* send this storm into my life?" My prayer is that this book will answer these questions with hopeful and faith-filled theology and with the eternal wisdom that is found only in the Word of God.

We must recognize that not only does a storm have the power to introduce us to God, but it also has the capacity to introduce us to ourselves! When you are caught in a vicious downpour of circumstances, people, and events, you will discover exactly who you are and what you believe.

To me, the saddest aftermath of a violent storm is when a Christian loses their way in life. Storms often test the faith and peace of the storm-tossed victim, so that they come out of the ordeal weary and undone, with no discernible direction. I pray that, in every chapter of this book, you will find strength and joy to help you stay on track spiritually—or, if you have lost your way, to find the route back to your loving heavenly Father.

Uncommon Comfort

I have divided *StormProof* into seven parts, with each section covering a specific storm in the Bible. Each part is then divided into manageable chapters. The storms are not given in chronological order of their appearance in the Bible but, rather, in an order that I thought would be most advantageous to understand and learn from. So, don't allow the sequence of the storm presentations to throw you; instead, just soak in the lessons from each tempest.

This book is meant to be a weather forecaster, an umbrella, a compass, and a storm shelter for you. Ultimately, *StormProof* presents the uncommon comfort that is available only from biblical principles—offering the shelter of faith, hope, and love. The Bible does, indeed, possess an umbrella of protection for any storms looming on the horizon of your life. As a believer in Jesus Christ, you are able to access the hiding place that is found by those who are more captivated by the Savior than by the storm.

Finally, my prayer is that by studying the simple yet timely principles presented in these pages, you will begin to realize that a storm doesn't have to be your worst moment; instead, it can be your finest hour.

Then they cried out to the LORD in their trouble, and he brought them out of their distress. He stilled the storm to a whisper; the waves of the sea were hushed. They were glad when it grew calm, and he guided them to their desired haven. Let them give thanks to the LORD for his unfailing love and his wonderful deeds for mankind. —Psalm 107:28–31 NIV

PART ONE

Remember the Last Miracle

ONE

The Calm Before the Storm

Most stories in life don't really begin at their beginning—at least, not at what we might identify as the beginning. The beginning could probably be defined as "the particular time when something noticeable happens or changes." Instead, often, events converge and build to create "beginnings." The same applies to storms. There are facts, events, and details related to a storm that precede its actual occurrence, and these may determine its ferocity and impact. Consider how atmospheric conditions shift prior to an ominous storm, and how they often determine the strength and length of the tempest, the temperature fluctuations involved, and the potential damage it may inflict.

The "calm before the storm" is one of those atmospheric changes that has a parallel in our personal and professional lives. It is often deceiving and can unfortunately lead us into a state of complacency—right before we are hit by one of the biggest blasts of our life! Such was the case in the following account, which has become one of the most famous "storm stories" in Bible history. That is why, before we study this particular storm,

27

we should examine the events that happened immediately prior to it. Of course, I could just tell you the story of the storm itself and leave the previous events untold. But then you would lack that proverbial (and resounding) "rest of the story" that is vital to understanding its significance for us today. The Holy Spirit has woven that significance into the biblical record so that people of all succeeding generations might understand its timeless meaning.

To begin before the beginning of the storm story, we must witness the miracle that preceded the tempest. I can guarantee you that observing the spiritual atmosphere that ushered this storm into human experience will be captivating.

It's Not About Me

Now when Jesus heard about John [the Baptist], He withdrew from there in a boat to a secluded place by Himself; and when the people heard of this, they followed Him on foot from the cities.
—Matthew 14:13

To set the scene here, Jesus had just received the news that His cousin and childhood companion, John, had been senselessly murdered. He needed a place of seclusion and solitude to process the human pain of loss and grieve the life of His dear friend and ministry coworker. But He could not get away by Himself even in this time of tragedy. The crowds were able to sniff Him out and discover the location of His quiet place.

When He went ashore, He saw a large crowd, and felt compassion for them and healed their sick.   —Matthew 14:14

This verse clearly demonstrates the heartfelt concern for others that Jesus lovingly chose to embrace at this moment of pain. He had wanted to be alone because He was in mourning, but mercy triumphed over grief.

Jesus knew that even during one of His life's darkest hours, He was on planet earth to heal the lives of broken and diseased people.

Exercising mercy will always lead to loving and compassionate ministry, while giving reign to selfishness will often drive us to seclusion. There comes a time during our dark days of grief and mourning when we must lay aside our solitude and reach out to others. *God cares about people—* this message never changes. Jesus, the Son of God, made the most of every opportunity, even when, in His humanity, He yearned to spend time alone with His Father. If you are desperate for a personal miracle, you might start by putting aside your own feelings and interests in order to reach out in compassion and mercy to others who are needy.

When someone is in pain, don't just talk...listen with your heart.

When someone has a need...meet it.

When someone is sick...pray for them and take them a meal.

Facts, Faith, and Future

When it was evening, the disciples came to [Jesus] and said, "This place is desolate and the hour is already late; so send the crowds away, that they may go into the villages and buy food for themselves." —Matthew 14:15

The disciples were just so human, weren't they? They definitely were not chosen to be disciples due to their giant faith or all-consuming compassion; these boys had so much to learn!

The disciples began this confrontation with Jesus by telling Him where He was—as if Jesus had not yet recognized the fact that He was in a *"desolate"* place! And then, this naive band of brothers informed the One who had left eternity and entered willingly into the limitations of time that the minutes were ticking by. They told Jesus, the living Word of God, who participated in creation as His Father flung the sun, moon, and stars into place, that the hour was getting late. Time was God's idea, yet these micro-managers were compelled to point out the obvious.

It was like telling Einstein that 2 + 2 = 4.

It was akin to showing Beethoven where middle C is on the piano.

It was similar to instructing Rembrandt in how to draw a stick figure.

And finally, these brilliant specimens of humanity told God, who was living among them in the flesh, how to handle a difficult situation. The God who has plans for our welfare and not for our calamity (see, for example, Jeremiah 29:11) didn't need the advice of a motley group who walked by sight and not by faith! (See 2 Corinthians 5:7.)

The disciples were focused on their lack—what they did not have—rather than on *who* was with them! They were fact-oriented, but Jesus always calls His disciples out of the temporal facts of a situation and into a place of faith in His character and in His power to demonstrate eternal realities. The disciples were consumed by their circumstances, while Jesus was consumed by the Father's compassion for the multitudes who had come to listen to, and receive from, His life-giving words.

In effect, what these assertive and thoughtless young men were saying to Jesus was this: "You have preached and ministered way too long today. We are going to have a hungry mob on our hands!"

Due to the atmospheric conditions they faced, the disciples were paralyzed by the situation and began to be critical about what they saw with their natural eyes. When well-meaning disciples of Jesus Christ—in any era of history—decide to walk by sight and not by faith, it will cause them to become frustrated with the Lord; then, often, these misguided disciples will begin to tell Jesus what to do. But, believe me...God *does not need our advice.* Telling Jesus what to do and apprising Him of situations and circumstances is just not necessary. The God of creation does not need your personal weather forecast!

The disciples had chosen to walk by sight; but Jesus, walking by faith, saw what they had missed—He saw the makings of an exciting miracle.

It did not matter that the hour was late and there was no fast-food restaurant on the corner. What mattered to Jesus in that moment was an opportunity to demonstrate the compassion and power of God. If you long for a demonstration of heaven's power, then don't look at what you have or don't have. *Look at what God has.* Don't look at where you are. *Look at who is with you.* Don't tell God what "time" it is. *Live from an eternal perspective.*

You can choose whether to walk by faith or by sight regardless of the threatening storm that looms on the horizon of your life. You can choose faith or you can choose to panic; you can choose to trust the Father to protect you or you can choose to spout negativity. You choose.

God's Opinion

But Jesus said to them, "They do not need to go away; you give them something to eat!" —Matthew 14:16

Jesus rarely agrees with our human answers to difficult and challenging situations. You should never expect Him to agree with your human appraisal of events, because He simply does not look at life the way most human beings do. Most of us see only the frustrations, while God sees only His answers to our frustrations. Yet, tapping into the wisdom of God, Jesus decided to include these faithless, fact-filled men in the answer to this dilemma of lack. He could have provided the necessary food without them, but He chose to involve them in the miracle. Jesus is still doing the very same thing today, nearly two thousand years later. He is still inviting faithless, fact-filled men and women to partner with Him in the miraculous.

If you are dealing with a situation that is rife with lack and poverty, begin to give yourself away to others. Giving is where the miracle always begins. If you face a storm today, remind yourself of these words that God spoke to Abraham thousands of years ago: *"I will bless you,…and so you shall be a blessing* [to others]" (Genesis 12:2).

"Only" Is Not in Heaven's Dictionary

They said to Him, "We have here only five loaves and two fish."
—Matthew 14:17

The disciples were able to produce *"only five loaves and two fish,"* which a young *"lad"* in the crowd had brought with him. (See John 6:8–9.) However, the word *only* is not in Jesus's vocabulary. It never has been and never will be. He does not know what an "only" is because He is the God of abundance. *Only* is the word of humanity, while *abundant* is the word of divinity. When you allow Jesus to be involved in your life, you can trust that every "only" that you face is certain to be touched by the miracle of His abundance.

And [Jesus] said, "Bring them here to Me."   —Matthew 14:18

Bring all of your "onlys" to Jesus and wait with grand anticipation as you discover what will happen when He touches an "only" with His abundance. "Only" is merely enough to feed one young boy, but when "only" is touched by Jesus, it becomes enough to feed a ravenous, frustrated, demanding, and tired mob!

Three Keys to a Miracle

Ordering the people to sit down on the grass, [Jesus] took the five loaves and the two fish, and looking up toward heaven, He blessed the food, and breaking the loaves He gave them to the disciples, and the disciples gave them to the crowds.   —Matthew 14:19

In this amazing verse, we find three keys to a miracle that reinforce the insights we have been gleaning from this storm story. Watching the life, hearing the words, and imitating the actions of Jesus on this particular day are what it takes to participate in a miracle at a moment of frustration and lack:

1. Look up!

You will never partner with Jesus in a miracle if you see only what is in your hands. You must set your gaze on heaven's power and remind yourself that there is a God who does, indeed, intervene in the affairs of human beings. There is a God who is more than enough in any of your life situations. There is a God!

2. Bless!

As you partner with Jesus in bringing a touch of heaven to earth, begin to pray and give thanks. Worship with your whole heart, knowing that God is well able to match His abundance with your "only," resulting in a miracle. Worship is the petri dish where miracles are conceived, and worship stimulates the atmosphere where miracles thrive and grow!

3. Start to Give!

Generosity is the fertilizer for a miracle conceived in the soil of worship. A miracle is not about what you have or do not have at your disposal to selfishly keep and hoard; instead, a miracle is about what you choose to give. When you decide to give what has been placed in your hands, you reveal the heart and character of God—and a miracle may be only moments away.

It is clear that Jesus deeply desired not just to perform a miracle for the people, but also to have the disciples be actual contributors to that miracle. He wanted to release them from the limited mind-set of walking by sight. Likewise, if all you are doing is reciting your problems, you will never experience the miraculous. You must partner with God in lavish giving if you desire to watch the miracle begin with what is in your own hands. Those *"greater works"* (John 14:12) that Jesus promised we would do will be merely an elusive and hoped-for dream unless we choose to give away what we already have.

Give, and it will be given to you. They will pour into your lap a good measure—pressed down, shaken together, and running over. For by your standard of measure it will be measured to you in return. —Luke 6:38

I have learned the tender yet enormous truth that there are three distinct impossibilities in the life of a believer:

1. You will never be able to out-love God.

2. You will never be able to out-dream God.

3. You will never be able to out-give God.

Achieving any of these is humanly impossible. But when we love God and are intent on living abundantly in Christ, we will try to do all three out of our devotion to Him! It is when we endeavor to out-love, out-dream, and out-give God that our lives display a rich and rare abundance that most people can only imagine.

I dare you to try it—then watch the miracle that will take place in your very own hands, in front of your very own eyes. Spend the rest of your life trying with all of your might to out-love, out-dream, and out-give God!

"All"!

And they all ate and were satisfied. They picked up what was left over of the broken pieces, twelve full baskets. —Matthew 14:20

Do not make the sad mistake of reading this spectacular verse only as history. Read it personally. Read it enthusiastically! Let's look at the verse again, allowing its truth to sink into the empty places in our lives:

And they all ate and were satisfied. They picked up what was left over of the broken pieces, twelve full baskets.

What! Are you kidding me? Surely you jest, dear Holy Spirit! These fact-chained boys did not merely hand out hors d'oeuvres to the crowd. They did not offer only a meager lunch of peanut butter and jelly sandwiches. This was a bona fide, miraculous, Thanksgiving feast. There would be leftovers for days—all because Jesus was there. Note that there were twelve basketfuls of food left over, one for each of the twelve disciples. Perhaps Jesus smiled as He handed one full basket to each of His astounded disciples and made the miracle personal for them. Let's imagine what He might have said.

To the disciple who was a former tax collector: "Matthew, just try to count what is left over in these baskets!"

To the disciple whose would later become known for his doubts about Jesus's resurrection: "Thomas, can you believe it? Leftovers!"

To the disciple who would later declare through the Father's revelation that Jesus is the Messiah: "Peter, what does this miracle say about who I really am?"

To the disciple whose life would become infused with the theme of God's love: "John, see this demonstration of My abundant love for all people!"

A Gargantuan Blessing

There were about five thousand men who ate, besides women and children. —Matthew 14:21

Theologians and historians believe there may have been as many as twenty thousand people there that day who were fed on five little rolls of no significant size and two dried-up fish. May I just remind you again that if you are only looking at what is in your hand (in your life), you will experience continual frustration and frequent fear. However, if you will look up to heaven, if you will choose to worship the great I Am, and if you are determined to be extravagant in your giving, the blessings that will come back to you will be gargantuan! There will be no way to measure the enormous miracle that will occur, because there will be leftovers in abundance. The miracle is never found in the size of the loaf—it is always found in the power of the Lord who is with you.

"The most incredible thing about miracles is
that they happen."

—G. K. Chesterton

TWO

Help Is on the Way!

At this point in your reading, you might be wondering, "When we are going to start studying the storms in the Bible?" Wonder no longer, my friend, but read on. Prepare to be drenched!

Time on the Mountain

> *Immediately [Jesus] made the disciples get into the boat and go ahead of Him to the other side, while He sent the crowds away. After He had sent the crowds away, He went up on the mountain by Himself to pray; and when it was evening, He was there alone.*
>
> —Matthew 14:22–23

Directly after the miracle of the loaves and fish, Jesus compelled the disciples to get into their boat and go across the Sea of Galilee. The crowds had been pressing in on Him. In fact, a parallel account in the gospel of

John tells us that, at this moment, the people even wanted to make Him king. (See John 6:15.) Jesus, however, sent the people away because He desired to go up to the mountain to pray.

Finally, after a long day of dealing with opinionated disciples and the needs of the multitudes who had followed Him around, Jesus was at last able to go to the mountain to pray. He still longed for extra time with His Father that day as He processed the death of His cousin John the Baptist.

Never underestimate the healing power of being in the presence of your heavenly Father as you process the things that cause you grief and sadness. If Jesus, who was perpetually in fellowship with the Father, needed time alone with Him, how much more do we need to spend focused time with Him! Jesus ached for these powerful moments of intimacy with His *"Abba"* (Mark 14:36), and so should we. The problem with us is that we try to fill our spiritual or emotional ache by seeking earthly solace in such things as entertainment, recreation, shopping, and food. Yet nothing will comfort you like time spent on your knees in God's presence. When you are sorrowful or grieving, temporarily remove yourself from everyone and everything else in your life and make it a priority to go to the "mountain" to pray.

Finally...a Storm

And now the moment has come for which you have been patiently waiting—the storm is about to hit! Are the disciples ready for it? Has the recent gargantuan miracle prepared these valiant and chosen young men to be fortified against the winds and waves that are about to blow their little boat off course? How will these starry-eyed disciples respond to an epic blast?

What a Boat!

But the boat was already a long distance from the land, battered by the waves; for the wind was contrary. —Matthew 14:24

Oh, how I love this little boat! I wish I could have just one piece of splintered wood from this vessel that was rocked to and fro by the *"contrary"* winds of nature. Perhaps this was the boat Peter had used as a fisherman before the Lord called him with the words *"Follow Me"* (Matthew 4:19). Perhaps, before reaching the shore where the multitude had gathered, this little boat had soaked up the tears Jesus had cried after hearing about the death of His beloved cousin, who had "made a way in the wilderness" for Him. (See, for example, Matthew 3:1–3.) Jesus might even have taught from this little boat, sitting in it just off the shoreline so the boisterous crowds could hear His voice. (See Luke 5:1–3.) Now, this little vessel—which, for some of the disciples, represented their former occupation of fishermen—is about to encounter a storm that has been remembered over the course of two thousand years.

There are three significant facts to observe from Matthew 14:24 as we begin to view the makings of another miracle:

1. The boat was a long distance from land.

2. The boat was in the midst of a contrary wind.

3. The boat was being battered by the waves.

Due to circumstances in your life, you may be experiencing conditions similar to those this little wooden boat did at that moment in history. Perhaps you feel you are in the midst of a driving and contrary wind, your life has run off course, and you are not where you think you should be. Now, you have been left battered by these negative events. You might even be experiencing the tremendous strain of a life torn apart by relentless trials. You wonder if anyone understands how far away from stability and security you seem to have wandered. You may question if the Lord even knows where you are and if He is aware of what kind of storm you are encountering! You might feel certain that if something does not stop the storm soon, you will be fighting for your very existence. You are crying out, even now, "What if things never change? What if this storm never relents!"

Divine Instruction

And in the fourth watch of the night He came to them, walking on the sea. —Matthew 14:25

The fourth watch of the night is between three and six in the morning. The disciples had been battling this vicious storm for perhaps as long as twelve hours and their options for safe passage to their destination had run out. You may be in the "same boat": you may be exhausted from having fought the effects of the winds and waves in your life beyond what seems humanly possible.

The last time the disciples had encountered a storm of this magnitude, Jesus had been in the boat with them (see, for example, Matthew 8:23–27), but this time, they were on their own—or so it seemed.

When Jesus was on the mountain communing with the Father, maybe He was praying for this group of a dozen disciples whom He had chosen. Perhaps He was hoping that these men who insisted on walking by sight and not by faith had learned a lesson or two by now. Maybe He had been hoping they would remember the words He had spoken the last time they had been caught in the middle of the sea by a tumultuous storm:

"Peace, be still!"   —Mark 4:39 NKJV

"Why are you afraid, you men of little faith?"   —Matthew 8:26

But that day, during this new storm, I don't think these disciples— who had seen food supernaturally multiplied, people miraculously healed, and other storms calmed—were recalling those miracles. Instead, I suspect they may have been asking questions like these:

"What if we drown?"

"What if our boat splits apart?"

"Where is Jesus? Why didn't He come with us!"

During the storms in our lives, we will ask either faith-filled questions or fearful, pitiful ones. Storms have a tendency to go to the heart of our issues and pull up either doubt and disappointment or faith and hope.

And remember, these disciples were in the direct path of this particular storm simply because they had obeyed Jesus. They were there by divine direction. The Lord had placed them in the path of this immense, killer storm. There is no storm this side of heaven that is a surprise to the One who made the winds and the waters.

Why would a good and loving Father place His dearly loved children in such a storm? That is actually an easy question to answer.

First, He would place them in hurricane-like conditions in order to perform a miracle! When God, the all-wise Father, allows one of His own to encounter a serious atmospheric plunge, it is often to bring glory to His name. If you are in a storm today, consider the idea that maybe, just maybe, you are right where God wants you to be. I believe that His purpose for allowing a storm is also to remind His children that life is about more than the temporal things we often become absorbed in. Life, in its fullness, is about our absolute dependence upon Him.

Second, He would place His children in a storm to increase their trust in, and dependence upon, Him—the One who rules the winds and the waves.

So, don't let the direction of your circumstantial winds intimidate you, because you may be in exactly the right place at exactly the right time! Sometimes, it is obedience to the heart and words of Christ that will usher us into the path of a storm. Just because events and people are coming against you does not necessarily mean you are doing—or have done—something wrong. Don't ever walk away from obeying the Lord just because the winds are contrary. If the loving Father of creation has allowed you to experience a storm, He is also going to show you His eternal and matchless glory.

He Can See You!

When we read the account of this storm from the gospel of Mark, we glean even more exciting and powerful details about it:

Immediately Jesus made His disciples get into the boat and go ahead of Him to the other side to Bethsaida, while He Himself was sending the crowd away. After bidding them farewell, He left for the mountain to pray. When it was evening, the boat was in the middle of the sea, and He was alone on the land. Seeing them straining at the oars, for the wind was against them, at about the fourth watch of the night He came to them, walking on the sea; and He intended to pass by them. —Mark 6:45–48

The disciples in this dear little boat were over three miles away from the safety of the coast from which they had sailed. The natural eye is unable to see three miles away, especially with the added challenge of stormy winds and ferocious torrents of rain. Yet, although the disciples could not see Jesus, He could see them! He saw His men *"straining at the oars."* He saw the minute details of what they were doing in the middle of this violent storm. Likewise, in the middle of your crisis, Jesus knows right where you are, He knows what you are doing, and He knows what it will take to get to you.

The disciples were working hard at doing the right thing, humanly speaking, under the circumstances of this violent storm—trying to keep the boat from capsizing under the onslaught of wind, waves, and precipitation. Continuing to do the right thing is a personal challenge for all disciples of Christ in their trials. Let me encourage you to keep doing what is right, because Jesus sees you! Stay focused on the task at hand while anticipating His arrival and help during your tempest. Don't become discouraged, no matter how hard the wind blows or how high the waves roll. Even when you are unable to see anything ahead of you because of the strength of the storm, remember that God is aware of what you are doing—and help is on the way!

Jesus Comes...He Always Comes

In the fourth watch of the night, Jesus began His miraculous approach to these young men whose lives were being endangered by their circumstances. At this point, the disciples had been in the boat for nearly twelve hours, battling the near hurricane-force winds. Notice that Jesus came walking toward them on the very substance that was threatening to overwhelm and kill them! Similarly, He is not intimidated by your circumstances but is able to use your storm as the vehicle for His approach.

The sea was foaming and frothy; the violent waves were rolling back and forth, rocking the boat from side to side, and yet Jesus came. Knowing that a fierce storm was on the horizon, Jesus could have kept His disciples on dry land—but He chose not to do so. Or, He surely could have calmed this monstrous storm from the shoreline; one word from the Man who created that puddle, and it instantly would have been still—but He chose not to do so. Instead, He chose to show up *in the midst of* the howling wind and brutal waves. The God who created the elements is certainly not intimidated by them. Jesus did not yet calm the turbulent and agitated waters but, rather, walked across them!

A Cakewalk

When Jesus strode toward the storm-tossed and weather-beaten boat, this was no short, easy jaunt but about a three-mile hike across angry, tempestuous waters. He was undoubtedly covered with the spray of the water and by particles of sand driven by the wind. And yet He kept walking.

This is what we must grasp when we are in the throes of any storm:

What is impossible for man is a cakewalk for God.

What causes us to fear is a stroll in the park to Him.

What we are overwhelmed by, He controls!

Jesus made steady progress across the roiling, turbulent water. He was probably drenched to the bone, but even then, He did not calm the sea. Nevertheless, I imagine He had one thought in mind: "I must get to My boys!"

> *When the disciples saw Him walking on the sea, they were terrified, and said, "It is a ghost!" And they cried out in fear.*
> —Matthew 14:26

Jesus will often come in a manner that it is difficult for us to understand from a human perspective. And sometimes, in the middle of our out-of-control emotions, we mistakenly accuse Him of being something or someone that He is not. Remember, although the waves were endangering the lives of the disciples, Jesus used those same waves as the vehicle upon which He walked into their storm. They never expected that! There are people whom we dread and circumstances we fear, and unfortunately our response to them is often to succumb to our flailing emotions. However, it is through what we fear the most that the greatest blessings of our lives can come if we will recognize Jesus's lordship over all.

The Arrival of the Great I Am

But immediately Jesus spoke to them, saying, "Take courage, it is I; do not be afraid."
—Matthew 14:27

The great I Am has arrived! I Am has appeared on the scene of this epic blast. When Jesus saw that the disciples were afraid, He did not correct them, nor did He discipline them. He encouraged them. And still, Jesus had not calmed their storm. The tempest continued to rage out of control and create a monstrous threat to their lives.

In the same way, before Jesus deals with the storm of your life, He will first confront your fear issues. Jesus has come to you in the storm to bring you His courage! He wants you to be more aware of His presence than you are of the tempest that is hurling you around. When you are being battered by a contrary wind, the first miracle that happens is the gift of His peace, which is pronounced over your life as a result of His dear presence.

My friend, know that in the midst of your raging and brutal storm, Jesus will come to you. You might not recognize Him at first, but He will, indeed, come because He has promised that He will never leave you or forsake you. (See, for example, Hebrews 13:5.)

"Remember no storm lasts forever. Hold on. Be brave. Have faith. Every storm is temporary and we're never alone."

—Author unknown

THREE

The Right Question

The questions that one asks while in the middle of a storm are a powerful determinate of one's ability to survive the storm. When you are in the middle of a storm, what types of questions do you ask? Those questions might just determine your potential to overcome the tempest. Let's consider the question Peter asked when Jesus arrived in the middle of that storm at sea.

> Peter said to [Jesus], *"Lord, if it is You, command me to come to You on the water."* —Matthew 14:28

The Underlying Meaning

Peter began this unforgettable meeting and conversation with Jesus by asking an interesting question. He phrased it in the form of a statement, but it was really an inquiry. Peter—the man who would eventually have the audacity to rebuke Jesus for saying He would die on a cross (see, for example, Matthew 16:21–22) and would cut off someone's ear in an attempt to keep His Lord from being unjustly arrested (see, for example, John 18:10)—just wanted to know one thing in the middle of this relentless storm: "Lord…is it You?"

He didn't ask, "Lord, where have You been?"

He didn't query, "Lord, what if another wave comes crashing this way?"

He didn't demand, "Lord, what if this little boat breaks apart?"

He didn't think to ask, "Lord, what if we never make it to shore?"

And he didn't verbally speculate, "Lord, what if we all die!"

Instead, this impetuous companion of the Savior merely wondered, "Lord, is it really You?"

Perhaps that is the question we should all ask at the worst moment of our life's storms: "Jesus, is it You?"

I love Peter. He is my favorite disciple. I have often prayed, "Lord, when I am in a storm, give me the faith of Your buddy Peter." What is left unsaid here is the underlying meaning behind Peter's inquiry. Perhaps what Peter intended everyone in the little wooden boat to comprehend was what the nearness of Jesus offered for all of them:

"Jesus, if it's really You, that means that a miracle is about to take place!"

Isn't it amazing that even in the middle of a ferocious and uncontrollable storm, Peter desired to do what Jesus was doing? He longed for the miraculous power of Jesus to be demonstrated in his own life and in his own humanity. In this instance, at least, Peter was the only one of the twelve disciples who seemed to want the *"greater works"* (John 14:12). He was the only one who possessed the bravado to ask for a miracle to occur. The other disciples in the weakened boat were apparently wiping their brows and taking one another's blood pressure. Perhaps they were reminding one another, "Breathe in…breathe out…breathe in…breathe out." Maybe some of these men were seasick due to the rocking of the boat. It's reasonable to believe that the disciples not only had to try to navigate a storm outside their boat but also maneuver across a deck spotted with slippery vomit!

But Peter, the man of adventure and faith, recognized this moment as the opportunity of a lifetime. He knew he could be part of a demonstrative miracle of Jesus, and so he proclaimed, in effect, "Jesus, I want what You've got!"

What you say in the midst of a trial is a revealer of your character and desires. Perhaps it will be in the worst storm of your life that your deepest desire is revealed. This storm revealed that Peter boldly desired to be like Jesus.

Not one other disciple had dared to speak a word yet. They were listening to this exchange that was taking place between Jesus, the Miracle Worker, and Peter, one of their leaders.

"Come!"

> And [Jesus] said, "Come!" And Peter got out of the boat, and walked on the water and came toward Jesus. But seeing the wind, he became frightened, and beginning to sink, he cried out, "Lord, save me!"   —Matthew 14:29–30

Jesus had still not calmed the storm, and yet Peter got out of the boat and began to walk across the vicious waves as he imitated the very actions of Jesus.

The modern church has often been very critical of Peter at this moment of his life because he took his eyes off of Jesus and sank in the waters. It is true that he did, indeed, take his eyes off of Jesus. But let me hasten to point out these facts to those of us who are quick to criticize him:

Peter, the common man, walked on the water with Jesus, the Son of God, superseding the laws of nature.

Peter, the uneducated (but opinionated) fisherman, used tempestuous waves as literal stepping-stones to reach his beloved Lord.

Peter, the one who would deny Christ three times, accepted Jesus's invitation to "Come" to Him outside of a boat in the middle of a storm at sea!

Have you ever done that? I didn't think so....

Yet, when Peter started looking at his circumstances, he saw the force of the wind, and he became frightened. And the instant he took His eyes off Jesus and became more aware of the storm than he was of his Savior, he began to sink. It is clear that if you are more aware of your personal squall than you are of the presence and power of Jesus, like Peter, you will become overwhelmed with fear and find that you are in way over your head. What will hold you up on the rolling waves is your faith. What will keep you from drowning in the middle of your monsoon is an awareness of the One who is with you. The Man who made the seas has more than enough power to calm those waters! The waves still answer to the sound of His voice. Never confuse where the absolute power lies: it lies not in the storm, but in Him.

The Twinkle in His Eye

Immediately Jesus stretched out His hand and took hold of him, and said to him, "You of little faith, why did you doubt?"

—Matthew 14:31

Jesus is always ready to catch us when we falter. He is always ready to save us, despite the strength of the storm in which we find ourselves. He is always ready to protect us, regardless of the size of the waves threatening our lives. Peter never should have taken his eyes off of Jesus, but when he did, at least he quickly corrected himself with the words that millions of others have cried: *"Lord, save me!"* (Matthew 14:30).

"Jesus, save me!" might be the most effective prayer to pray when you have taken your eyes off of the Lord. It is when you are in a storm, gripped by panic and fear, that you should look for His almighty hand and then stretch out your own hand to meet His capable and caring grasp. Jesus is actually very good at saving disciples who are in over their heads. Maybe it's because He has had to do it so often.

We might read the phrase *"You of little faith, why did you doubt?"* and wonder if Jesus was upset with Peter, or, at the very least, frustrated with him. But I have often wondered if Jesus's eyes were twinkling as He reached out His hand to catch one of His dearest friends. Perhaps He was indicating, "Pete! I gotcha! Didn't you know that I would catch you? We have to work on your faith, brother!"

The instant Peter reached out and took the hand of Jesus, he was up on the waves again. My weathered friend, even if you have made devastating and unforgettable mistakes in life, take Jesus's hand! If you have had a faith crisis of your own making, take His hand! Look into His twinkling eyes and cling to Him with every ounce of strength that remains in your storm-tossed life!

At Last, the Storm Is Stilled

When they got into the boat, the wind stopped.

—Matthew 14:32

Only when Jesus and Peter got back into the boat did the wind finally stop its persistent howling. Wherever the presence of Christ is known and recognized, the wildest storm must cease. No matter how long your storm has raged and how violent your circumstances have become, Jesus is not ignoring your tempest. He is on His way and will, indeed, calm your storm in His perfect and complete timing.

And those who were in the boat worshiped Him, saying, "You are certainly God's Son!"   —Matthew 14:33

Every storm you experience in life should culminate in sincere worship that reflects a greater understanding of who God is. One of the benefits of raging tempests is that they can help you to recognize His nature and qualities in a way that the easy, sunny days of life are not able to. When the winds stop howling, and they will...and the waves cease crashing, and they will...and the boat stops rocking, and it will...spend time in complete adoration of the One who speaks peace to your every storm. Never leave the storm behind without offering heartfelt praise to Him and declaring for the world to hear who you know Him to be.

Then, the next time you are in the middle of a howling storm, you can declare to that storm the truth of who Jesus is!

Remember the Last Miracle

Then [Jesus] got into the boat with them, and the wind stopped; and they were utterly astonished, for they had not gained any insight from the incident of the loaves, but their heart was hardened. —Mark 6:51–52

Every time I read this passage written by the Holy Spirit and Mark the evangelist, my heart seems to stop within my chest and I find myself on my knees in God's presence. There is a detail hidden here that never ceases to cause me to perform a necessary self-examination regarding my memory: *The disciples had not learned anything at all from observing the miracle of the loaves and fish.* Their hearts were so hard that they had developed spiritual amnesia concerning what the Lord was capable of doing on their behalf. I don't ever want to develop spiritual amnesia. I want my faith to be led and strengthened by all that God has done for me in my life.

I sincerely hope you never find yourself in over your head, surrounded by seaweed and dangerous waves, but if you do, remember the loaves and the fishes. The compass that will lead you out of the storm is your ability to recount the miracles God has done for you and others in the past. The miraculous God of the land who provides for us in abundance is also the God of the seas who preserves our lives in times of peril.

If you have been a Christian for longer than twenty-four hours, I am sure you have tasted the goodness of the Lord! When you are in a storm—or during any adverse and unwelcome conditions—recall His goodness and feast on His faithfulness. Remember your last miracle, or time of divine comfort, and praise Him for certain victory, even as the winds are blowing and the waves are crashing out of control.

"There are some things you can only learn in a storm."

—Author unknown

PART TWO

Unexpected and Undeserved

FOUR

Where Are You, God?

Have you ever been in a storm that was created by the actions or accusations of others? Some storms seem grossly unfair, decidedly undeserved, or quite unjustifiable; the damage caused by these particular tempests seems especially appalling and reckless. Paul, the great champion of the gospel of Jesus Christ, found himself in such a storm. From this tempest, we can extract life-changing principles that will enable us to make it through our own unexpected and undeserved storms. Let's dig in!

The Eye of the Miraculous

Paul had been arrested for obeying the injunction of Jesus Christ and preaching the hopeful message of salvation. After having made his defense before King Agrippa and the Roman governor Festus, Paul was being sent to Rome because he had appealed to Caesar. He was placed on a ship—the fastest means of transportation of the day for long-distance travel—along with other prisoners who were being sent to Italy. This ship, with its crew, soldiers, prisoners, and cargo, would take Paul on the first leg of his journey as he traveled all the way from the eastern to the western Mediterranean. Here is what happened, as narrated by Luke, the author of the book of Acts and Paul's coworker in the gospel.

When it was decided that we would sail for Italy, they proceeded to deliver Paul and some other prisoners to a centurion of the Augustan cohort named Julius. And embarking in an Adramyttian ship, which was about to sail to the regions along the coast of Asia, we put out to sea accompanied by Aristarchus, a Macedonian of Thessalonica. The next day we put in at Sidon; and Julius treated Paul with consideration and allowed him to go to his friends and receive care. —Acts 27:1–3

Paul had two traveling companions on this unwarranted journey: Luke and Aristarchus. Roman law permitted that Roman citizens under arrest, which Paul was, were allowed to take with them one or two slaves to care for their personal needs. Many theologians suggest that Luke and Aristarchus volunteered to serve as Paul's compassionate slaves. Luke may actually have signed on as the ship's doctor. Paul, being tried unfairly, was now on a dangerous trip, and yet these two men refused to leave his side. Their love for the apostle must have been enormous, because they were willing to endure the indignity of being treated as slaves, as well as the perils of sea travel. These men made great sacrifices to ensure Paul's safety and to enable him to continue to preach the gospel.

What sacrifices have you made for the gospel of Jesus Christ? It is a question that deserves an answer, whether the conditions of your life are stormy or placid. Many believers prefer comfort over courage. Rather than face a potential storm, we hide snugly in our twenty-first century Western comfort zone and mind-set. We assuage our consciences by asserting vague consolations, such as "Surely the Lord wouldn't call me away from the life I am currently living!"

But Luke and Aristarchus left convenience and advantage on the shores of Caesarea and embraced the bravery that a tumultuous sea voyage necessitated. They chose to sail away from the mundane and into the eye of a miraculous future because of their devotion to God and his minister Paul. God deeply desires to use men and women who determine that mediocrity will never be a part of their weather forecast!

More Contrary Winds

From there we put out to sea and sailed under the shelter of Cyprus because the winds were contrary. —Acts 27:4

It wasn't long into the journey before the vessel hit winds that were *"contrary."* (Sound familiar?) Contrary winds on the ocean often signal the threat of an even larger storm. This sailing ship made a wise decision to seek shelter around the coast of Cyprus. Cyprus is an island on the eastern side of the Mediterranean ocean. Rather than head into the open sea when the sailing conditions were so unstable, the ship hugged the shoreline of the safest place it could find.

Likewise, when contrary winds come storming against our journey in life, one of the first and most important things we must do is to discern the safest possible place to sail toward for shelter. However, as noted earlier, at such times, we often choose to cling to things that have no safety value at all. We choose temporary pleasures such as shopping or eating, and when we find that those choices have no power against hazardous spiritual, emotional, or physical conditions, we begin to emote our disappointment or blame others.

The only shelter that will protect you from the winds of negative circumstances and the gales of trauma is the shelter of Jesus Christ. We all know that our only truly safe place is Jesus—but do we choose to shelter there? Do you choose Jesus when your life is sailing through perilous winds and jeopardous waters?

"Choosing Jesus" during a storm season in life simply means to go to Him rather than seeking solace in the media, creature comforts, or other distractions. Sailing under the shelter of Jesus is the choice of reading your

Bible and allowing the eternal words on the sacred pages to serve as the compass for your soul. You will find respite from the contrary winds of life when you worship rather than whine. "Trust Jesus" is not a mere pat answer or colloquialism of Christianity but a vibrant decision guaranteed to turn your life toward the safety of His *"everlasting arms"* (Deuteronomy 33:27).

Of all the choices that are yours to make at a juncture of ferocious circumstances or hostile treatment from other people, choose the safest place to weather the storm. Emotions have no saving power, materialism will only mislead you, and the prevailing cultural answers will merely give a false sense of security. Therefore, choose wisely and choose quickly— choose the true Shelter. His name is Jesus.

"But let all who take refuge in You be glad, let them ever sing for joy;
and may You shelter them, that those who love
Your name may exult in You."

—Psalm 5:11

FIVE

A Horrible Season

*When we had sailed through the sea along the coast of Cilicia
and Pamphylia, we landed at Myra in Lycia. There the centurion
found an Alexandrian ship sailing for Italy, and he put us aboard
it. When we had sailed slowly for a good many days, and with
difficulty had arrived off Cnidus, since the wind did not permit
us to go father, we sailed under the shelter of Crete, off Salmone;
and with difficulty sailing past it we came to a place called Fair
Havens, near which was the city of Lasea.*   —Acts 27:5–8

There are seasons in life when conditions may seem to go from absolutely terrible to entirely debilitating. Such was the situation in which Paul
found himself in the middle of the Mediterranean Sea. Under the guard
of the centurion, Paul, his companions, and the other prisoners had been
transferred to a second ship, which was heading for Italy.

This ship's progress was also hindered by unremitting winds. Day after day after day, the crew found themselves the victims of a vicious gale that nearly paralyzed them in their attempts to reach their destination. A strong "nor'wester" forced this storm-battered boat along the southern coast of Crete, where it arrived at Fair Havens. The bay of Fair Havens earned its encouraging name (a translation of the Greek *Kaloi Limenes*) from the protection it provided against northwestern winds.[1] Fair Havens still exists as a port today.

Remember that this account of Paul's stormy journey was placed in the Bible to show those of us who are living today how to navigate through the storms of our lives. In this part of the journey, we are reminded again that preservation during a monstrous storm depends entirely on the availability of shelter.

I don't believe that anything is in the Bible by mistake or by chance; in my view, every name, date, and biblical account holds a piece of eternal encouragement for the children of God. If the forecast of your life has been seriously impacted by the relentless winds and choppy waves of your personal environment, hold on to hope, because "Fair Havens" may be just up ahead to give you respite during your dangerous journey!

We have been blessed with the most inviolable refuge and the most unassailable sanctuary in all of eternity. Run to the "Fair Havens" of your soul today and find your security in Him.

Deliver me, O Lord, from my enemies; in You I take shelter.
—Psalm 143:9 NKJV

Walk by Faith, not by Forecast

When considerable time had passed and the voyage was now dangerous, since even the fast was already over, Paul began to

---

1. Todd Bolen, "Fair Havens, Crete," *BiblePlaces.com*, accessed November 17, 2018, https://www.bibleplaces.com/fair-havens/.

admonish them, and said to them, "Men I perceive that the voyage will certainly be with damage and great loss, not only of the cargo and the ship, but also of our lives." —Acts 27:9–10

The Roman calendar for this particular year, AD 59, places this leg of Paul's rough and stormy voyage when *"the fast was already over."* The *"fast"* refers to Yom Kippur, or the Day of Atonement, which took place on October 5 that year. Most ships would sail on the Mediterranean Sea during the summer season of May to early September. Experienced sailors and ship captains knew that sailing from the east to the west after mid-September was "iffy" at best—and became suicidal by early November.

The vessel on which Paul was traveling was a rudderless boat steered by two huge paddles and propelled by a gigantic, square mainsail. While the ship was state of the art, it was still unable to handle the fierce winds that continued for many weeks. Paul's ship was attempting to sail during a time that was quickly becoming the most dangerous and frightening season of the year to travel by sea.

Could it be that you have been paralyzed by a "stormy season" that has not permitted you to move forward in fulfilling your destiny? Perhaps you believe that your life is unable to handle any more stress or damage than you have already sustained. Maybe you wonder if you can make it through yet another disappointment, criticism, rejection, or month of bills. You might even wonder if you will live through this monstrous storm.

The God who guided and protected Paul through his undeserved yet dangerous storm is the same God who guides and protects you through the tempests of your life. Remind yourself that the Lord is *"the same yesterday and today and forever"* (Hebrews 13:8). Cease focusing on the storm and the potential damage that may ensue and set your gaze firmly on Jesus, the One whom the winds and waves must obey. (See, for example, Matthew 8:27.) Quickly and continuously remind yourself that the gales of circumstances and the waves of tumultuous relationships must submit to His Word and will. The Lord has the miraculous ability to bestow supernatural peace even in the midst of the worst squall of your life. His peace is not dependent upon your circumstances but upon His presence. He has promised never to leave you and never to forsake you (see, for example, Hebrews 13:5), even when you experience gusting disappointments and torrential downpours of discouragement.

Especially during the stormy days of life, we must determine to walk by faith, and not by sight, by sound, or by forecast! (See 2 Corinthians 5:7.) Walking by faith is the decision to place all of your hope and all of your trust in the God who is working all things together for your good and for His glory. (See Romans 8:28.) A storm holds no decision-making power in the kingdom of God; even in life's distressing times, remember that all power and authority have been given to Jesus. (See Matthew 28:18.) The safest thing to do during the worst tempest of your life is to dig into the Bible and find God's perspective on your storm! When you can't trust your own judgment, trust the One who is the Author of all truth.

A Sudden Change

But the centurion was more persuaded by the pilot and the captain of the ship than by what was being said by Paul. Because the harbor was not suitable for wintering, the majority reached a decision to put out to sea from there, if somehow they could reach Phoenix, a harbor of Crete, facing southwest and northwest, and spend the winter there. When a moderate south wind came up, supposing that they had attained their purpose, they weighed anchor and began sailing along Crete, close inshore. —Acts 27:11–13

During this period in history, ships were navigated by the stars because compasses had not yet been invented. Paul had warned the captain and the other officers of the ship that the overcast skies and powerful winds made sailing west at this time the worst possible decision they could make. He had made his opinion known that to continue the voyage could result in considerable damage and even in the potential loss of their very lives. Prior to this journey, Paul had already survived three shipwrecks (see

2 Corinthians 11:25), so perhaps he was merely giving them the wisdom of his own common sense. However, the majority of those on the ship, including the ship's officers, did not listen to his warning.

The weather conditions had eliminated any possibility of reaching Italy that year, and so the captain's plan was to reach Phoenix and spend the winter there. When the wind moderated just a bit, the captain proceeded with the journey. If these favorable conditions had remained, the ship might have reached its destination within hours—but suddenly everything changed!

What Do You Do?

Before very long there rushed down from the land a violent wind, called "Euraquilo"; and when the ship was caught in it and could not face the wind, we gave way to it and let ourselves be driven along. —Acts 27:14–15

The air currents abruptly altered, and the resulting windstorm that blew down from the mountains of southern Crete became deadly. Luke used the Greek word for "typhoon" to describe this monstrous wind. This was a sudden, unexpected, and unwelcome change in the voyage of the ship, which was now bobbing along the Mediterranean like a small cork in a gigantic tempest! All they could do was just be driven along by the dreadful gale.

The truth is that we all experience sudden changes in the circumstances of our lives. There are moments when everything seems peaceful and calm, and then, suddenly, a disturbance of epic proportions blows in. May I just submit to you that rather than merely be driven along by the acute conditions that will endeavor to hijack your life, chart your course carefully before you encounter the next "Euraquilo."

Before a storm attacks your peaceful existence, determine that even in the middle of an undeserved tempest, you will continue to hold on to the Word and worship the One who made the winds and the waves. Decide prior to financial troubles that you will keep tithing and even give above your tithe, regardless of a scarcity of income. Establish the fact that you will continue to be kind even when others are cruel and negative. Resolve to forgive those who have pounced on your life with unwarranted accusations. Elect to continue to serve the Lord wholeheartedly even when the tentacles of depression surround your soul. Make a commitment that no matter what your health prognosis might be, you will remain a joyful, vibrant Christian who is filled to overflowing with the fruits of the Holy Spirit!

If you wait for the next "Euraquilo" to determine the course of your life, it is likely that you will run aground on the rocks of compromise or be carried away by the rapids of situational ethics. Face the contrary winds and allow the power of the Holy Spirit to fill the sails of your life! The Spirit is well able to guide you past any dangerous reefs and through any disastrous storm to your destination.

"I have learned to kiss the wave that throws me against
the Rock of Ages."

—Charles H. Spurgeon

SIX

Violently Storm-Tossed

Running under the shelter of a small island called Clauda, we were scarcely able to get the ship's boat under control. After they had hoisted it up, they used supporting cables in undergirding the ship; and fearing that they might run aground on the shallows of Syrtis, they let down the sea anchor and in this way let themselves be driven along. The next day as we were being violently storm-tossed, they began to jettison the cargo; and on the third day they threw the ship's tackle overboard with their own hands.

—Acts 27:16–19

Luke's vivid description of this high-powered, life-threatening storm makes me taste salt water in my mouth as I hold on to the rigging for dear life! I can feel the boat rocking turbulently under my feet as this morning's breakfast threatens to come back up.

There will be times when you will be unable to control the events that are rebelliously gusting into your life. During those moments, as you taste the saltiness of fear and as you hang on to anything that seems stable, always remember you have an Anchor.

Your security is found in clinging to a relationship with Jesus Christ. When the salt water of circumstances leaves a slimy aftertaste in your mouth and when the world around you is threatening and inconsistent, find your Anchor and let Him hold you fast amid the uncontrollable waters of your life.

The Blizzard of 2014

My husband, Craig, and I lived for many years just outside of Buffalo, New York, which has understandably earned the reputation as the "Snow Capital of America." We learned to hunker down during those lake-effect snow thrillers that last for days and just enjoy the safety of our own home and cozy days in front of a warm and inviting fireplace. However, during the second week of November 2014, we experienced a blizzard that threatened the safety and the future of the wonderful life we had been embracing.

I had been diagnosed with aggressive breast cancer on November 3, 2014, and spent the next week in offices and medical facilities being examined, poked, prodded, scanned, X-rayed, and biopsied. I bravely tried to sprinkle the joy that was mine on every person who was involved in determining what the treatment plan would require. Their lives were daily filled with women just like me who were being unexpectedly ushered into the battle of their lives, but for me, this was an unwelcome first. To my knowledge, no one in my family had ever battled cancer prior to my diagnosis. I was a healthy woman in the prime of life and was looking forward to celebrating the empty-nest years with my husband after decades of raising and homeschooling five children. The cancer storm had blown in and I didn't like it. I didn't like it one bit.

I was scheduled to see the breast surgeon and the oncologist on the morning of Tuesday, November 11. At this appointment, Craig and I would learn how they would treat the cancer that had angrily invaded my otherwise healthy body. However, on the evening of November 10, a lake-effect blizzard blew into the entire western New York region, and all roads were closed. The doctor's office called and said that they had rescheduled my appointment for November 26, the day before Thanksgiving.

What! I had to wait two weeks before I could see my doctor again? Didn't they know that the cancer might travel to other regions of my body if we waited for two unending weeks?

What I was unable to see in the whiteout conditions of my frigid circumstances was that God was giving me the precious gift of time in the middle of the storm to let down my Anchor.

The blizzard outside of my windows continued for five days and left over seven feet of snow in its wake. Roads were impassable for nearly another week as the residents of Erie County dug out from the worst blizzard in nearly four decades. Snug in my home and thankful for warmth and a stocked freezer, I discovered the power of focusing only on the Anchor and not on the storm.

I spent my days reading the Word and choosing verses to memorize. I filled a small journal with Scriptures that gave me strength and filled my heart with faith and joy. I made a list of "Fighting Scriptures" that prepared me for battle and a list of "Healing Scriptures" that solidified my faith.

I listened to worship music without ceasing and allowed the melodies of the great hymns of the faith to fill every corner of my spacious house. I made playlists of instrumental sacred songs and often played them all night in my home and in the various hospital rooms I would occupy.

I prayed on my knees every day for hours, and I rejoiced in the One who heals and restores. I went to the Great Physician for His opinion on my prognosis, and He gave me a joyful prescription of abundant life!

I spoke with friends from near and far and asked them to pray for me and to place my name on every prayer list they knew of. I consulted with respected family members and wise mentors as I kept my eyes set on the God of miracles.

I never would have chosen the storm that I was encountering, but the Anchor of my soul was sure and kept my life from being pitched with fear or driven upon the rocks of doubt.

Jettison the Extraneous

Luke reported that in the midst of the great storm that Paul and his fellow travelers were experiencing, *"they began to jettison the cargo"* (Acts 27:18). When that decision didn't lighten their load sufficiently, *"they threw the ship's tackle overboard with their own hands"* (verse 19).

The only way to keep the ship from sinking was to lighten the load by throwing everything extraneous overboard. The desperate crew had no choice but to dump all of the cargo that was not necessary for the saving of their boat or of their very lives. The next day, they determined that if they were going to make it through this typhoon, they must rid the ship of even the tackle supplies. These were frantic last rites for a dying ship, indeed!

In my own life, following several surgeries for cancer—after one of which I nearly died—months of vile drugs, and horrific treatments, I decided that it was time to begin to jettison my life's cargo. I needed to change my life in order to make it through this cancer cyclone and suffer no residual damage.

I chose to honor God in my temple, or body (see 1 Corinthians 6:19), which He had given to me to use while I am this side of heaven. My oncologist told me kindly, "If God made it and man hasn't messed with it, you get to eat it." That has been my motto now for nearly four years. I began to eat a clean and healthy diet, ridding myself of all sugars, processed foods, and soy products. I lost nearly fifty pounds in this jettison.

I also stopped dyeing my hair and using chemicals on my skin. I changed all of my makeup to that which was free of soy and cancer-causing chemicals. I even changed my toothpaste and deodorant to brands that were all natural and chemical free. The throwing-off has not been easy, but it has been wonderful!

What changes do you need to implement in order to steer clear of the rocky coastline you are being tossed toward and make it through your storm unscathed? What might you need to jettison out of your life? Every smart sailor knows the wisdom of doing this; every experienced seaman figures out what to dump overboard if they want to make it safely through a blasting tempest. Do you need to change your relationships or your spending habits? Do you need to cut up some of your credit cards or start cleaning up your schedule? Often, the storms we experience reveal quite clearly what needs to go. Ask God to show you what you need to discard in order to live a life that is free of avoidable, hazardous conditions. Don't be afraid to rid yourself of unhealthy habits, extraneous relationships, or "stinking thinking."

Don't hesitate another minute—begin to jettison now!

Keep Up Your Courage

Since neither sun nor stars appeared for many days, and no small storm was assailing us, from then on all hope of our being saved was gradually abandoned. When they had gone a long time without food, then Paul stood up in their midst and said, "Men, you ought to have followed my advice and not to have set sail from Crete and incurred this damage and loss. Yet now I urge you to keep up your courage, for there will be no loss of life among you, but only of the ship. For this very night an angel of the God to whom I belong and whom I serve stood before me, saying, 'Do not be afraid, Paul; you must stand before Caesar; and behold, God has granted you all those who are sailing with you.' Therefore, keep up your courage, men, for I believe God that it will turn out exactly as I have been told. But we must run aground on a certain island." —Acts 27:20–26

Can you picture this episode in your mind's eye? Can you even imagine what Paul and the other inhabitants of this sailing vessel were facing? Some of them had probably tethered themselves to anything stable in order to prevent being washed overboard. They clung to any object that was fastened to the deck of the ship and spit out salt water as yet another giant wave washed over the side of their storm-tossed sloop. Almost everyone on the ship—the crew, the passengers, the prisoners, and the slaves—was demoralized. They had lost all hope that this storm would ever end; and even if it did, would they live to tell about it?

In the middle of this dark and desperate scene, Paul stood up to address everyone. I picture him covered in sticky salt water as he began a sermon that has not lost its power to encourage us during our personal storms!

Paul, who had endured so much for the gospel of Jesus Christ, told these frightened and waterlogged individuals, *"Keep up your courage"*! What power-packed and authoritative words coming from a man who had given up creature comforts and safety because of his deep love for Jesus. In the following passage from 2 Corinthians, read what Paul recounted about his life:

Are they servants of Christ?—I speak as if insane—I more so; in far more labors, in far more imprisonments, beaten times without number, often in danger of death. Five times I received from the Jews thirty-nine lashes. Three times I was beaten with rods, once I was stoned, three times I was shipwrecked, a night and a day I have spent in the deep. I have been on frequent journeys, in dangers from rivers, dangers from robbers, dangers from my countrymen, dangers from the Gentiles, dangers in the city, dangers in the wilderness, dangers on the sea, dangers among false brethren; I have been in labor and hardship, through many sleepless nights, in hunger and thirst, often without food, in cold and exposure.

—2 Corinthians 11:23–27

Paul is my personal hero! What a champion of the faith and sacrifice for the cause of Christ! I deeply desire to embrace his heart and perspective as my own—I want all of his faith and all of his courage. Paul wasn't threatened by, or afraid of, the storm, because he was more aware of the strength of God than he was of his own weakness. He once wrote,

And [God] has said to me, "My grace is sufficient for you, for power is perfected in weakness." Mostly gladly, therefore, I will rather boast about my weaknesses, so that the power of Christ may dwell in me. Therefore I am well content with weaknesses, with insults, with distresses, with persecutions, with difficulties, for Christ's sake; for when I am weak, then I am strong.

—2 Corinthians 12:9–10

Paul had been praying in the midst of this storm and listening for the voice of God. What a great example he has set for us! Quit panicking and begin praying. Stop complaining and start petitioning. Cease worrying and begin worshipping.

During the tempest, Paul prayed not only for himself, but also for his fellow desperate travelers. This is yet another example of Paul's personal greatness in the midst of difficulty. When you find yourself in a raging storm, pray and listen for God's response. Hang on to His presence with every fiber of your being as you align with His heartbeat. Then intercede for others!

Even though he was still a prisoner, Paul became a combination of admiral and cheerleader to the group of weary voyagers. He emerged as a leader who spoke with the voice of hope. Now remember, the reason the Holy Spirit included this exciting seafaring story in the Bible was so that you and I could extract life principles from Paul's adventures. The apostle's words echo through the millennia of history as he charges all believers in Jesus Christ with the resolution to "keep up our courage"—even when we are experiencing the worst storm of our lives!

The next time you are in a storm, become the voice of hope to those around you. You might be the solo voice of hope, but start cheering other people up. Quit talking about the storm and start speaking about your God. Humanity and history have no idea how much they owe to the presence of righteous men and women in the middle of devastating circumstances.

Choose Brave

Cancer is just plain hard, and it turned into the worst storm of my life. Like Paul, I had experienced other devastating circumstances in my nearly six decades of life, but none had become a "Euraquilo" like this dreaded disease. In my thirties, I had walked through seven years of clinical depression. I had suffered from years of infertility. I had to release five babies to heaven who were born too early—four of them I held in my hand. Yet nothing had rocked my security like cancer did. I was in a battle with the enemy for my very life and, like Paul, I was determined to stay courageous and steadfast.

As the months of my cancer battle turned into nearly two years of intense treatment and surgeries, I maintained my determination to be brave. I knew that I had access to the power of the Holy Spirit and that nothing was impossible with God. I was determined to allow the Lord to use me, even if I was having needles stuck into my body or was lying on an operating table. I was resolute that I would not waste this opportunity to take the joy of the Lord to the darkest places imaginable—oncologists' offices and the cancer wards of hospitals.

One night, while my husband and I were lying in bed during the horrific battle, reviewing our life together and the battle we were in, Craig said to me, "Carol, you are the bravest person I know." I felt the tears begin to roll of out the corners of my eyes and I whispered to him in the dark, "When brave is your only choice, you choose brave."

When Courage Is Hard to Find

Yes, Paul's words echo through the centuries as a riveting reminder of how to endure the instability of a life storm: *"Keep up your courage"* (Acts 27:22). Paul did not only urge this response one time in his powerful soliloquy, but he repeated it: *"Therefore, keep up your courage, men, for I believe God that it will turn out exactly as I have been told"* (verse 25). If you forget every other principle in this book, remember this one: Keep up your courage!

Where does a person find courage when the wind is wailing and the visibility is nearly zero? Where does courage come from when an ordinary man or woman is in the middle of a downpour of disappointment or a deluge of despair? Where is courage in that moment?

Hidden in Paul's words is a four-word phrase that holds the key to courageous living: "For I believe God…" (verse 25).

You will never embrace the potent attribute of courage if you don't first begin by believing God. Even if your heart denies that belief, let your lips confess it. When your blood pressure is rising, let your faith take over and declare loudly enough for the winds and the waves and the demons in hell to hear, "I believe God! I believe that He is good and that He is with me!" In that moment of declaration, fear will take a back seat to courage. Courage will then be at the helm of your ship and will guide you through the fiercest onslaught that life can imagine.

Let me tell you what courage is:

+ Courage is the dynamic choice to believe the eternal fact that God is always good and that He will, indeed, have the final say in every storm. (See, for example, Psalm 34:8.)

+ Courage is the conviction that He is our shelter and "a very present help in trouble" (Psalm 46:1).

+ Courage is the resolute certainty that He will never leave you or forsake you. (See, for example, Deuteronomy 31:6.)

+ Courage is the mind-set that God has been to your future and that it is good because He is good! (See Jeremiah 29:11.)

+ Courage is tying yourself to the promises of God and never letting go of them! (See, for example, 2 Corinthians 1:20.)

+ Courage is steering your mind away from worry and choosing to walk by bold faith, unswayed about by you see in the natural. (See, for example, Philippians 4:6–8; 2 Corinthians 5:7.)

Men and women throughout all of recorded history have had to make the choice to be brave when their defenses were down and their very worlds were imploding. You are not the only human being who has ever had to make the choice to be brave. We are the children of the King of the ages, and He has given us His Holy Spirit so that we might choose to be brave even in the fiercest storm or the hottest fire—even when we find ourselves "between the devil and the deep Red Sea."

"Disturb us, Lord, to dare more boldly, to venture on wider seas where storms will show Your mastery; where losing sight of land we shall find the stars. We ask you to push back the horizons of our hopes; and to push into the future in strength, courage, hope and love."

—Author unknown
(sometimes attributed to Sir Francis Drake)

SEVEN

The Good News and the Bad News

But when the fourteenth night came, as we were being driven about in the Adriatic Sea, about midnight the sailors began to surmise that they were approaching some land. They took soundings and found it to be twenty fathoms; and a little farther on they took another sounding and found it to be fifteen fathoms. Fearing that we might run aground somewhere on the rocks, they cast four anchors from the stern and wished for daybreak.

—Acts 27:27–29

Paul and his maritime companions had spent over two weeks in the "storm of the century" when, finally, they heard some breakers upon the land. However, this actually wasn't the solution that you might suppose it would be.

The good news was that they were close to land! I can almost hear this weathered crew breathe a collective sigh of relief. But then came the inevitable realization of the bad news. The bad news was...they were close to land! I can imagine the stress that suddenly intensified in their hearts as they grasped that they might be dashed upon the rocky coast and the storm-battered boat be broken into smithereens! It was obvious that they needed to approach the coast at daybreak so they could be in better control of the type of landing they would experience. What did this crew of tired, waterlogged men do? *"They cast four anchors from the stern and wished for daybreak."*

That one phrase holds all the wisdom that you will ever need for any treacherous and long-lasting storm in life. According to the translators of the *New American Standard Bible*, in the Greek, the last part literally reads, "They were praying for it to become day." When you feel as if your life is about to be battered upon the shores of your circumstances, *cast four anchors deeply and then wish—rather, pray—for daybreak!* This amazing, seaworthy advice has stood the test of time through the two thousand years that have passed since Paul spent a fortnight in a typhoon.

Advice from a Contemporary Seasoned Sailor

This account of Paul's confrontation with a monster of a storm and the perilous rocks reminds me of a story I read several years ago in a book by one of my favorite authors, Max Lucado:

> Labor Day weekend 1979....
>
> While the rest of the nation played, the Gold Coast of south Florida watched. Hurricane David was whirling through the Caribbean, leaving a trail of flooded islands and homeless people....
>
> On the Miami River, a group of single guys was trying to figure out the best way to protect their houseboat. Not that it was much of a vessel. It was, at best, a rustic cabin on a leaky barge....

It was like a *McHale's Navy* rerun. They bought enough rope to tie up the *Queen Mary*. They had their boat tied to trees, tied to moorings, tied to herself. When they were through, the little craft looked as if she'd been caught in a spider's web. They were so busy tying her to everything, it's a wonder one of the guys didn't get tied up.

How was I privy to such a fiasco? You guessed it. The houseboat was mine.

...I had owned the boat for three monthly payments, and now I was about to have to sacrifice her to the hurricane! I was desperate. *Tie her down!* was all I could think.

I was reaching the end of my rope, in more ways than one, when Phil showed up. Now Phil knew boats. He even looked boat-wise.

He was born wearing a suntan and dock-siders....

He felt sorry for us, so he came to give some advice...and it was sailor-sound. "Tie her to land and you'll regret it. Those trees are gonna get eaten by the 'cane. Your only hope is to anchor deep," he said. "Place four anchors in four different locations, leave the rope slack, and pray for the best."[2]

"Anchor deep...and pray for the best" sounds like familiar and brilliant advice to me! But what are the anchors? You will never make it through the storms of life—and believe me, there will be storms—unless you know what your four deep anchors are.

Here are my four anchors. I have touched on these areas previously, but I want to teach you how to make them deep anchors in your life to hold you secure amid your stormy circumstances. I will always use these specific anchors through each and every tempest in my own life. Whether I am

_____

2. Max Lucado, *Six Hours One Friday* (New York: W Publishing Group, 2012), 1–2.

facing depression, cancer, financial challenges, or rejection, I will anchor deep and pray for the best!

Four Deep Anchors

Anchor #1: The Word of God

The first anchor that protects my life from the jagged shoreline of circumstances is the Word of God. The eternal truth, divine wisdom, and inherent healing power that are found on the sacred pages of the Bible determine my primary anchor of protection.

When I was battling cancer, just a few days into my storm, I cried out to God, asking Him for a "fighting verse" that would give me strength for all that lay ahead of me. On that ordinary yet momentous day, when I looked at my Bible-reading plan, my assignment was to read in the book of Nahum. Now, let's be honest here, many people don't even know there *is* a book in the Bible called "Nahum"! It's an obscure work, hidden among the Minor Prophets in the Old Testament. But that day, the inspired truth of a prophet named Nahum gave me the necessary strength for such a storm as I was facing.

After praying, I opened my Bible to the first chapter of Nahum and began to read; when my eyes reached the last verse of that chapter, I knew that I had found my anchor:

For never again will the wicked one pass through you; he is cut off completely. —Nahum 1:15

Because I had taken the time to ask the Lord for a specific verse, and because I had also actually taken the time to open my Bible, my anchor was deep! At every doctor's appointment, with every bad report I received, and in every moment my body was in pain, I was able to declare this truth from the Word of God: *"For never again will the wicked one pass through me; he is cut off completely"*!

Anchor #2: Worship

The second anchor that holds my life steady in the appalling monsoons of life is a choice to worship even in the storm. When the tempest is building force on the horizon of my life and the forecast is deadly—I choose to worship! When the waves of circumstances are threatening to wash over me and the riptide is threatening to pull me under—I choose to worship! When the shoreline is dangerously rocky and I am afraid for my very life—I open my mouth and sing!

Moses, Miriam, and the Israelites sang after watching the Lord defeat Pharaoh's army in the Red Sea, delivering His people from destruction. (See Exodus 15:1–21.) King David sang his way through depression. (See, for example, Psalm 30.) When the kingdom of Judah was being unfairly attacked by enemy armies, King Jehoshaphat appointed singers to go out before Judah's army, singing, *"Give thanks to the Lord, for His lovingkindness is everlasting,"* and God caused their enemies to destroy one another. The Bible actually recounts the fact that *"when they began singing and praising, the Lord set ambushes against the sons of Ammon, Moab and Mount Seir, who had come against Judah; so they were routed."* (See 2 Chronicles 20:1–34.) Three young Hebrew men in captivity in Babylon worshipped the living God even though they knew they would be thrown into a fiery furnace, and God miraculously preserved their lives. (See Daniel 3.) We should do no less by offering the Lord praise and worship during—and after—our own trying or dangerous circumstances.

My friend, stop murmuring or moaning—and start worshipping! The people of God are a people who sing; it is what we are known for. We sing when others weep and we worship when others complain. We praise when others panic and we make melody in our hearts when others allow dread to fill their souls.

So then do not be foolish, but understand what the will of the Lord is. And do not get drunk with wine, for that is dissipation, but be filled with the Spirit, speaking to one another in psalms and hymns and spiritual songs, singing and making melody with your heart to the Lord: always giving thanks for all things in the name of our Lord Jesus Christ to God, even the Father.

—Ephesians 5:17–20

The choice to throw the anchor of worship deeply into the waters that surround your life is a decision that every believer needs to make at their worst moment in life—will I sing or not?

GREATLY REJOICE!

We know that the apostle Peter encountered a storm or two in his life. These are his words of advice to those of us who are encountering rough waters:

In this you greatly rejoice, even though now for a little while, if necessary, you have been distressed by various trials, so that the proof of your faith, being more precious than gold which is perishable, even though tested by fire, may be found to result in praise and glory and honor at the revelation of Jesus Christ; and though you have not seen Him, you love Him, and though you do not see Him now, but believe in Him, you greatly rejoice with joy inexpressible and full of glory.

—1 Peter 1:6–8

In the course of these three verses, Peter twice exhorted his readers to *"greatly rejoice"*! Peter said that when life is at its worst, *"greatly rejoice"*! He reiterated that when your faith is being tested, *"greatly rejoice"*! Worship is an anchor of the soul when your world is falling apart—just ask Peter.

Worshipping in the midst of trials is a theme that runs throughout all of Scripture. For example, we read this in the book of Habakkuk:

Though the fig tree should not blossom and there be no fruit on the vines, though the yield of the olive should fail and the fields produce no food, though the flock should be cut off from the fold and there be no cattle in the stalls, **yet** *I will exult in the* Lord, *I will rejoice in the God of my salvation.* —Habakkuk 3:17–18

The greatest time to praise the Lord is when you have had the very worst week of your life. That is when you should lift your hands and declare, *"I will bless the* Lord *at all times; His praise shall continually be in my mouth"* (Psalm 34:1)!

A SONG IN THE NIGHT

The type of cancer that had invaded my breast tissues required several different stages of body-altering surgery. My gifted surgeon had to keep operating until he had "gotten it all." Actually, the cancer was never gone from my body until he removed both breasts entirely, as well as surrounding tissues.

If I learned nothing else in the pain-filled hours immediately following surgery, I learned to sing in the dark. I had a playlist on my phone that was filled with healing music, and how I loved listening to those beloved, specifically chosen songs that would aid in my healing process. But the most healing melodies of all came directly from those who were present with me and who loved me. Craig was always there during those difficult hours, as was my college roommate and dear friend Debby Edwards. Craig has a wonderful tenor voice and Debby is gifted with a beautiful, lilting soprano. My daughter Joy, the consummate alto, was often there, as was her college roommate, Cady, who minored in worship arts in college. They were quite the quartet and became very adept at singing away my pain!

After one particularly difficult surgery, they were gathered around my bed singing the great songs of faith that I have loved since childhood. They sang for hours...and hours...and hours. When one of them stopped to engage in some much-needed rest, I would beg, "Don't stop singing! I need you to sing!"

Finally, when their voices were hoarse and their bodies were about to drop, I said to them, "OK—if you can't sing anymore, then call Kelly!"

My sweet husband, who was holding my hand and had tears running down his cheeks, replied, "Honey, it is after midnight. Kelly lives in Ohio—I am not sure that I should call her this late."

And I, being the submissive wife that I am, demanded, "I don't care how late it is, and I don't care where she lives—call Kelly. She will sing to me."

And so he called Kelly, who was a dearly loved daughter in the faith to me. She had often traveled with me and led worship when I spoke at conferences across the nation. Kelly woke up from a sound sleep and sang over me for nearly two hours until I was able to fall asleep.

If you are in a storm, start singing—and keep singing! If you are unable to sing, beg someone else to sing over you.

Anchor #3: Prayer

My third anchor is a commitment to prayer. I have found it needful—more times than I can count—to stop talking about my storms and instead start praying about them. Why should I worry about the weather forecast when I serve a God who created the clouds, winds, and rain? Why should I cower in fear when my God can speak one word to a storm and cause it to cease in an instant?

Prayer is a place of powerful influence and sweet communion; prayer is the force that makes hell quiver in fear and causes heaven to rise to its feet and joyfully applaud. Eternal, heavenly realities are brought to earth through the participation of believers who are committed to the discipline of prayer.

I have heard it said that "history belongs to those who pray," and I know that to be true. Prayer is the vehicle through which the greatest work of any of our lives will be accomplished.

Therefore I say to you, all things for which you pray and ask, believe that you have received them, and they will be granted you.

—Mark 11:24

Storms have a way of convincing a believer to give up on the arena of prayer when, in reality, that is the time when we should pray the longest and the loudest. I defiantly refuse to believe that prayer is a waste of time but will set my resolve and continue to pray, even when nothing seems to change.

Be anxious for nothing, but in everything by prayer and supplication with thanksgiving let your requests be made known to God. And the peace of God, which surpasses all comprehension, will guard your hearts and your minds in Christ Jesus.

—Philippians 4:6–7

I will pray when the howl of life's storms endeavors to drown out the volume of my solitary and desperate prayer. I will pray when the storms rage on and the billows roll. I will pray in the dark of night when towering mountains threaten to minimize my value.

Pray without ceasing.   —1 Thessalonians 5:17

I will pray in the face of sickness and pain, and I will beg for God's sweet presence to heal and restore. I will refuse to be paralyzed or crippled by what my eyes see, and I will keep praying when others give up. I will pray in spite of a quiet heaven. I will wear out the carpet beside my bed, for there is no storm that can move me from this victorious battle position.

Then you will call upon Me and come and pray to Me, and I will listen to you. You will seek Me and find Me when you search for Me with all your heart.   —Jeremiah 29:12–13

I will arise early on a stormy morning with worship in my heart and with a stubborn prayer on my lips. I will choose to pray in faith rather than mumble with worry. I will lay my head down again at night with the comfort that any day is a magnificent day that has been given to prayer.

My calling is to prayer—while God's responsibility is to answer and to move. Although my prayers may not change a situation, I know they will change me. I have heard it said that God sometimes calms the storm, while He always calms His child. When I pray, Jesus is glorified in me and I am glorified in Him. When I pray, His grace is lavishly dispensed into my world.

Anchor #4: The Holy Spirit

My fourth anchor is the power of the Holy Spirit.

> *I will ask the Father, and He will give you another Helper, that He may be with you forever.... But the Helper, the Holy Spirit, whom the Father will send in My name, He will teach you all things, and bring to your remembrance all that I said to you.*
>
> —John 14:16, 26

The Holy Spirit has always been a part of God's plan for the believer's life, just as Jesus has been a part of God's plan for humanity since before the beginning of time. After His resurrection, Jesus promised that when He went to heaven to be with God the Father, He would send the Holy Spirit to be here on planet earth with us.

You will never make it through any storm in life, large or small, if you don't tap into the power of God's Spirit—and allow yourself to be changed by it! I have discovered that I am unable to get through even the peaceful, ordinary days of life without the Spirit's power.

RECEIVE...AND BE A WITNESS!

> *But you will receive power when the Holy Spirit has come upon you; and you shall be My witnesses both in Jerusalem, and in all Judea and Samaria, and even to the remotest part of the earth.*
>
> —Acts 1:8

The Greek word translated *"power"* in this verse is *dunamis*, from which we derive the English word *dynamite*. *Dunamis* can be translated as "explosive strength, ability, and power." The Holy Spirit is a Gift Giver extraordinaire, and He knows exactly what you need to make it through the storms of life.

As incredible as you are—because you have been made by God at this moment in history in order to live a significant and abundant life—you will be unable to accomplish anything at all without the Spirit's *dunamis* power. You have been especially created and redeemed to receive that power; *dunamis* is a perfect fit for your remarkable container.

The wonder of Acts 1:8 is found in the statements *"You shall receive..."* and *"You shall be...."* When you receive the power of the Holy Spirit, you become someone you could never be on your own. You need the power of the Spirit to enable you to walk in your calling and destiny in Christ. The Holy Spirit changes ordinary men and women into powerful witnesses for Christ and His kingdom. *Dunamis* changes wimps into witnesses and deniers into testifiers.

When Jesus was arrested by the authorities, all His disciples ran scared. (See Matthew 26:47–56; Mark 14:43–50.) After Jesus's arrest, Peter denied Him three times. (See, for example, Luke 22:55–62.) When Jesus was crucified, all the disciples except for John were absent. (See John 19:25–27.) Yet, after the Holy Spirit filled these fearful, intimidated men, it was said of them:

> *These who have turned the world upside down have come here too.*   —Acts 17:6 NKJV

Jesus knew that we who live this side of heaven's peaceful shores would never outlast a storm without the *dunamis* power of the Holy Spirit!

> *When the day of Pentecost had come, they were all together in one place. And suddenly there came from heaven a noise like a violent rushing wind, and it filled the whole house where they were sitting.*

And there appeared to them tongues as of fire distributing them-selves, and they rested on each one of them. And they were all filled with the Holy Spirit and began to speak with other tongues, as the Spirit was giving them utterance.　　　—Acts 2:1–4

The power of Pentecost was never meant to be a one-time spiritual high but a new way of knowing God, living for God, serving God, and being filled with God!

Isn't it interesting that the sound of the Holy Spirit at Pentecost is described as *"a violent rushing wind"*? That sound must have been tremendous! Although I have never heard the roar of a tornado, I have heard it likened to the sound of a fighter jet taking off or a huge freight train coming down the tracks. The mighty sound heard by the believers who were gathered in the upper room was loud enough, unusual enough, and perhaps terrifying enough that people in the surrounding area began to gather to find out what was going on.

The *dunamis* force of heaven had interrupted the disciples' formerly calm prayer meeting! The energy of heaven had broken loose around them, and the power of heaven was in their midst. They were walking in an atmosphere permeated with the courage and authority of heaven. If you are in a storm today, you desperately need your life to be invaded by this life-changing dynamism as well!

What happened next is the stuff of fantasy, but it is 100 percent historically accurate. The manifestation of the Holy Spirit not only sounded like a mighty, rushing wind, but it looked like fire. Luke described it as one hundred and twenty separate *"tongues as of fire,"* which rested on each believer. Not one person was left out—everyone heard the sound of the wind and received a tongue of fire upon them. John the Baptist had announced that Jesus would baptize His followers *"with the Holy Spirit and fire"* (see, for example, Luke 3:16), and this was the moment when that all began. *"And suddenly there came from heaven a noise like a violent rushing wind, and it filled the whole house where they were sitting. And there appeared to them tongues as of fire….*" I know this to be a scientific fact: when wind meets fire, it is inevitable that the fire will spread! Always!

After the wind and the fire, the third tangible sign of the *dunamis* power of the Holy Spirit was that believers began to speak with other tongues as the Spirit gave them utterance. Now, let me challenge you—don't read this account only in a historical sense, as you may have read it hundreds of times previously. Read this account as if you were in that very room.

Perhaps John looked over at Peter and opened his mouth to speak, planning to say, "Hey, Pete, you have fire on your head!" Yet instead of speaking in Aramaic, a different language came out that John had never before learned or studied, and perhaps had never heard.

Or, Mary might have glanced in the direction of her son James, intending to say, "What is happening in here? Are we safe?" But instead, out of her mouth flowed a torrent of words that were not of her natural vocabulary. Those words had absolutely no cerebral meaning for Mary, but out they came!

Even though the believers couldn't comprehend what the Holy Spirit had given them to speak, the words had meaning for the God-fearing Jews who had come from many countries and regions to worship in Jerusalem and were now gathered to listen to these extraordinary "*tongues*" that told—in their own languages—of "*the wonders of God.*" (See Acts 2:5–11 NIV.)

As far as we know, Jesus never spoke in a language that He didn't learn from His earthly parents or from a teacher. The disciples did, however, because this was the very first example of the "*greater works*" that Jesus said His disciples would accomplish. (See John 14:12.) At Pentecost, we also see the fulfillment of the words of Jesus when He promised, "The Holy Spirit is with you but will be in you" (see John 14:17), and "*When the Helper comes, whom I will send to you from the Father, that is the Spirit of truth who proceeds from the Father, He will testify about Me*" (John 15:26).

These, then, are four deep anchors that can preserve us in any storm: the Word of God, worship, prayer, and the Holy Spirit.

And so It Happened...

Now, let's return to Paul and his fellow travelers! What happened after the crew cast their four anchors and prayed for daylight? Daylight did come, and they indeed saw land—with a bay they might be able to reach—but as they made their way toward it, the ship struck a reef, and the vessel began to break up!

The soldiers' plan was to kill the prisoners, so that none of them would swim away and escape; but the centurion, wanting to bring Paul safely through, kept them from their intention and commanded that those who could swim should jump overboard first and get to land, and the rest should follow, some on planks, and others on various things from the ship. And so it happened that they all were brought safely to land. —Acts 27:42–44

To me, the most amazing words of this entire maritime story are found in the last sentence of the last verse of Acts 27: *"And so it happened…."* My heart is incredulous at the understated truth of these four words.

After this weakened sailing vessel hit a reef and began to be torn apart, all 276 passengers and crew (see Acts 27:37) either swam or found something to grab onto as the waves washed them upon the shore. They were alive, just as God had promised! They had all made it through the weeks of relentless, howling winds and torrential downpours!

The next time you are in over your head, think of Paul's sea journey and remind yourself that God will fulfill His promise to always be with you and carry you through.

"Life's roughest storms prove the strength of our anchors."

—Author unknown

PART THREE

An Epic Saga

EIGHT

Noah, the Ark, and God

Whenreading a book that covers significant storms in the Bible, you might have expected me to have started with the greatest tempest in the history of the world, that legendary torrent of epic destruction—the flood. However, I decided to tuck the gargantuan storm story of Noah and the ark until well into the body of this book. I made this decision for several reasons, but the primary one was that I didn't want my readers to be overwhelmed by the events that overwhelmed Noah. I didn't want to "flood" you with information, facts, and hard-learned lessons but rather allow you to slowly develop your storm mentality before we tackled this gigantic tempest.

But now, my friend, it is time—time to travel back through the millennia and enter the historic days before, during, and after the deluge. This is our moment to extract compelling lessons from Noah's culture, the ark that he built, and the God whom he served.

Back to the Beginning

Noah lived just ten generations after the time in which Adam and Eve lived. During this period in history, people lived for hundreds of years (Noah himself was six hundred years old at the time of the flood) and were able to give birth to dozens of children. Perhaps the reason for this was that God wanted the population to multiply quickly, and so He allowed His children, even though they were struggling with deep sin, to multiply and fill the earth.

At this pivotal moment, God looked down upon the people whom He had created, and He faced the difficult fact that only one man, Noah, was living a righteous life.

Then the LORD saw that the wickedness of man was great on the earth, and that every intent of the thoughts of his heart was only evil continually. The LORD was sorry that He had made man on the earth, and He was grieved in His heart. The LORD said, "I will blot out man whom I have created from the face of the land, from man to animals to creeping things and to birds of the sky; for I am sorry that I have made them." But Noah found favor in the eyes of the LORD. These are the records of the generations of Noah. Noah was a righteous man, blameless in his time; Noah walked with God. —Genesis 6:5–9

The previously perfect world that God had created for the benefit of humanity had been infested with evil thoughts, sin, and great wickedness. God had created these now sinful human beings for the express purpose of close and intimate fellowship with Him. The only way humanity has ever been able to walk in peace, joy, and fulfillment is by establishing a friendship with God. However, the world of Noah's day had become filled with people who ignored Him, ridiculed Him, and refused a relationship with Him. Although these people had been created in the very image and likeness of God, they were now alienated from their Maker—and were actually destroying themselves.

When I think of the culture in which Noah lived and read this historical account, the statement that nearly breaks my heart is this one: "*The* LORD *was sorry that He had made man on the earth, and He was grieved in His heart*" (Genesis 6:6). Don't those words just pierce your very soul? Let me remind you that one of the most powerful ways to read the Word of God is to read it personally rather than just historically or even theologically. This verse is like a microscope for our lives, and we must allow it to examine our own hearts, thoughts, words, and actions. It prompts me to ask myself, *What might I have done to grieve the Lord?* My selfish choices and opinions, based upon the world's belief system rather than upon the eternal and abundant truth found only in the Word, have the same potential to grieve the heart of the God whom I so love.

Also, when I ponder the world into which Adam and Eve were created and when I consider the marked difference between that atmosphere and the world in which Noah lived, the words of Genesis 1:31 become a sobering reminder to me of what God had accomplished at the beginning of time:

God saw all that He had made, and behold, it was very good.

In only ten generations, human beings had traveled the treacherous pathway from "*very good*" to causing God to "[grieve] *in His heart.*"

Taking a Walk with God

What does God do with His grief? I believe that, although deeply grieved by the attitudes and activities of sinful humanity, God always looks for one man or one woman who will simply walk closely with Him. Only ten generations after creation, He looked for someone on whom He could bestow His favor—and He found Noah. Righteous living is always a magnet for the favor of God.

For the eyes of the LORD *move to and fro throughout the earth that He may strongly support those whose heart is completely His.*

—2 Chronicles 16:9

The Lord searches in every generation and at every moment in history to strongly support His children who choose Him over everything else. You can be very sure that God is still looking today, as He did during the days of Noah, to find someone on whom He can lavishly apportion His favor. The blessing that comes from choosing to live a righteous life can never be overstated; it is always given to those who commit to walking with Him.

Every person during Noah's generation could have, and should have, made the same choices Noah did, but the sad reality is that no one else did. No one but Noah and his family chose the tremendous way of living that is offered to everyone by God the Creator. He offers His love, His friendship, and His forgiveness to all. However, just as in the days of Noah, not everyone today will respond to His offer.

The Adjectives of Noah

In the book of Genesis, Noah is described in this way:

Noah was a righteous man, blameless in his time; Noah walked with God. —Genesis 6:9

The fact that the Bible uses the words *"righteous"* and *"blameless"* to describe Noah does not mean that he never sinned; what it does mean is that Noah was a man who wholeheartedly loved God and quickly obeyed his Creator. Noah walked day-by-day, step-by-step, with the God who loved him and pursued him.

You and I live in the era that is known as "AD"—or after the historic life, death, and resurrection of Jesus Christ. And we who experience the joy of abundant living provided by Christ, the only begotten Son of the living God, apply a somewhat different meaning to *righteous* and *blameless*. Under the new covenant, to be righteous and blameless before God means we believe in Jesus as our Savior and Lord, we have repented of our sins, and we have asked God to forgive us for those sins. Because of that exciting request, we have now been cleansed by Jesus's precious blood, which

He shed on the cross for us, and we have received the indwelling Spirit of God. It means we are committed to following Jesus and are daily being conformed to His image. Like Noah, we walk with our God, who continues to love and pursue His people.

I can assure you that for any future storm in your life, as you remain in the righteousness of Christ, your heavenly Father will do for you what He did for Noah. He will give you a specific plan for how to live in a protected place during a storm, and He will be your shelter in that storm. Although Noah and his family had to endure the deluge, they were protected in the midst of it; your Father will do the same for you.

Is There Another Way?

*The LORD saw that the wickedness of man was great on the earth, and that **every intent of the thoughts of his heart was only evil continually**. The LORD was sorry that He had made man on the earth, and He was grieved in His heart. The LORD said, "I will blot out man whom I have created from the face of the land...."* But Noah found favor in the eyes of the LORD. —Genesis 6:5–8*

I have read the account of Noah in the book of Genesis hundreds of times and know what is going to happen next. Even so, every time I read it again, my heart cries out, "Please, God, don't destroy the earth! Not this time! Do You have to do it? Isn't there another way?"

But each time my heart begs God to change His mind about this already concluded historical event, it is as if I hear His gentle voice answering me, "If there had been a different way, I would have done it. How I longed for these people to choose Me rather than to choose wickedness and moral depravity! I pursued them, but they turned their backs on Me. And so, I chose to save the righteous Noah and his dear family."

The annals of biblical history should convince each of us living in the twenty-first century to trust completely in the God who made us and pursues us. Each account of a man or woman in the Bible who chose God rather than the compromise of their culture is a voice of encouragement that echoes through the centuries and calls us to follow the Lord as well. Do you remember the following verse, written by Paul and the Holy Spirit, which we read earlier?

> *For whatever was written in earlier times was written for our instruction, so that through perseverance and the encouragement of the Scriptures we might have hope.* —Romans 15:4

From the life of Noah, I am encouraged to walk with God before the storm comes into my world; I am instructed that there is a protective covering over those who wholeheartedly love and obey Him. And although the story of Noah is, in many ways, a human tragedy, I discover the word *hope* between every verse! I hear the Holy Spirit calling my name to live with reckless abandon for Christ and His kingdom.

Storm Warning

> *Now the earth was corrupt in the sight of God, and the earth was filled with violence. God looked on the earth, and behold, it was corrupt; for all flesh had corrupted their way upon the earth. Then God said to Noah, "The end of all flesh has come before Me; for the earth is filled with violence because of them; and behold, I am about to destroy them with the earth."* —Genesis 6:11–13

As we read this confirmation of the stormy forecast, we must remind ourselves that God had deeply desired to be in intimate relationship with human beings. From the beginning of time, He had designed a glorious earth that was meant to be enjoyed by humanity. He had a plan for our abundant life from the instant He breathed His very breath into the bones and flesh that became the first man. It was *we* human beings who rejected Him; it was His own creation who ignored their Creator. Therefore, it was necessary for God to start again—reserving the bit of righteous yeast that still existed on earth.

Storm Preparation

As you might recall, for many years I lived just outside of Buffalo, New York, on Lake Erie, and I often had to prepare for a vicious snowstorm. Whenever you hear a weather person on TV describing the treacherous conditions of a lake-effect snowstorm—that is my reality for nearly six months of the year! Consequently, I have become quite the expert at storm readiness. When a blizzard is predicted, I know exactly what to do and how to respond.

First, before the predicted whiteouts make their appearance, I make a run to the grocery store and stock up on necessary items to ensure that my cupboards and freezer contain enough "comfort food" to make it through the five to seven days that Craig and I might be snowed in and unable to leave our snug home. Vegetable soup, chili, baked potatoes, and beef stew are our foods of choice when a wintery squall is raging outside our windows.

My handsome, Southern-born husband makes sure there is enough wood for the fireplace, enough batteries for four flashlights, and enough matches for the candles that line our mantle should we lose our electricity during the storm. He also takes care to see that we have emergency supplies in our cars in case we are caught out in a winter squall; he places warm blankets, water bottles, granola bars, and an ice scraper within easy accessibility in my vehicle. Craig also scatters salt crystals along the driveway and up the sidewalks to help prevent ice buildup on our well-walked pathways. The finishing touch on our storm preparation is when I pick up my e-reader and download a new book or two to entertain me during the short days and long nights of the seemingly never-ending winter season.

Every impending storm in life requires similar determined and strategic preparation. God gave specific instructions to Noah so that he and his family would be kept safe from the impact of the flood that was about to come upon the earth:

Make for yourself an ark of gopher wood; you shall make the ark with rooms, and shall cover it inside and out with pitch. This is how you shall make it: the length of the ark three hundred cubits, its breadth fifty cubits, and its height thirty cubits. You shall make a window for the ark, and finish it to a cubit from the top; and set the door of the ark in the side of it; you shall make it with lower, second, and third decks. —Genesis 6:14–16

The Lord directed Noah to build an ark out of *"gopher wood,"* which many biblical scholars believe refers to cypress. Cypress is a light, yet extremely durable, hardwood. God's detailed blueprint for the ark included the architectural details of covering the inner and outer surfaces with pitch as a waterproof sealant, as well as directions for constructing the roof and the door on the side of the ship. The ark was a flat-bottomed vessel and had three decks, as well as various rooms to house people and animals and to store the amount of food this epic storm would require. A window lined the space just under the roof, providing necessary ventilation as well as light. God had thought of everything—as He always does!

Obey Anyway!

Here is an extremely interesting fact concerning the ark: the ship God commanded Noah to build was exactly six times longer than it was wide, which is the same ratio that is used by modern shipbuilders today. However, this massive houseboat was never intended to be navigated but was built only to float above the colossal waters that were about to cover the earth.

It took Noah and his sons a hundred and twenty years to build this floating zoo, which was the length of one-and-a-half football fields and as high as a four-story building! I imagine that they were mocked as they built the gigantic, wooden structure miles away from any ocean or lake. Who would build a boat large enough to house a family of eight and numerous animals when there was no water in sight? I believe the answer to this question is that people like Noah, who walk by faith and not by sight, are willing to obey the full instructions of God, take risks that the world doesn't understand, and always believe His promises.

Nevertheless, I wonder if even Noah scratched his balding head at times and wondered about the validity of this divine assignment. But, being a righteous man, he decided to continue to obey God's instructions rather than seek the applause of man.

Men and women of bold faith in every generation listen to the voice of the Lord and obey His meticulous directions even when it is impossible to understand, during the sunny days of life, the reason for His instructions. Audacious believers in God prepare for a storm even when the tempest has not yet begun to brew on the horizon of their lives. They heed the truths and principles of His Word as priceless instructions that have been given to aid us in storm preparation. God's Word is not arbitrary and contains no extraneous element that can be ignored. We must follow God's blueprint to the most minute detail in order to build a life that will last through the onslaught of any difficulty or trial. And, the wonder of it all is that when we share with our family members the directions God has provided, their lives can be saved as well.

Make It Personal

God asked Noah to build a gigantic boat in the middle of the desert that would take a hundred and twenty years to finish—what has God asked you to do lately? Perhaps He has reminded you to stay sexually pure until marriage or to love a difficult mother-in-law. Maybe He has invited you to stand up for truth in your community or to be a foster parent. God often asks of His children difficult things that are nearly impossible to understand with human reasoning, but I dare you to obey anyway.

Faith is not trusting God only when we understand what He has asked of us; it is trusting and obeying Him whether it makes sense to us intellectually or not—and this includes His instructions regarding imminent storms! It's okay to have some questions even as we obey. Faith is fertilized in the soil of questions and often thrives in an environment of thorns and rocks—as long as we are strongly grounded in our love and commitment to the Lord.

There may be times in life when we are mocked for our faith, when the world doesn't understand our righteous decisions, and when we are ridiculed for our purity. If this happens to you, continue to follow God's instructions rather than the call of a culture that does not recognize Him. It is God's deepest desire to prepare you for the storm that has been forecast in your life, but it is up to you whether or not you will prepare for it—and whether you will prepare God's way or your way. Noah and his family chose to ignore the mocking of their culture and to humbly and faithfully obey the Lord. The blessing would turn out to be epic.

"The eagle flies in storms while other birds seek shelter and other animals run and hide. With an adjustment of his wings, an eagle can fly almost motionless even in the face of great winds. The eagle uses the strong winds of the storm to lift him higher and higher until he rises above the clouds. The eagle has no power to stop the storm but he knows how to overcome it without fear."

—Kenneth Price

NINE

Have You Ever Seen the Rain?

Think about this for a moment: up to the time when Noah and his family were safely inside the ark, it had never before rained upon the earth. During the first ten generations of human beings, God had watered the earth by means of underground streams that provided the land with the irrigation it required. But now a cataclysmic downpour would fall from the sky, and gushing waters would be released from beneath the surface of the earth. Thus, the earth was about to experience something unique and unmatchable—something that has never happened again in human history.

There's a First Time for Everything!

Behold, I, even I am bringing the flood of water upon the earth, to destroy all flesh in which is the breath of life, from under heaven; everything that is on the earth shall perish. —Genesis 6:17

Don't you wonder what Noah was thinking at this juncture in his story? In his six centuries of living, he had likely seen many incredible wonders, but he had never seen rain. He had never observed one drop of moisture fall from the sky, and we can only imagine the fear that must have gripped his righteous heart as he pondered the colossal event that was about to take place. Noah's boyhood friends would all die in the storm; his neighbors and the village vendors would drown in the gruesome floodwaters. How could Noah begin to imagine what his life might be like after the destructive deluge?

However, into Noah's certain fear, God spoke these words of encouragement and promise:

But I will establish My covenant with you; and you shall enter the ark—you and your sons and your wife, and your sons' wives with you. —Genesis 6:18

God, the Father of all creation, personally invited Noah and his family to enter the ark, and He sealed the invitation with a promise. Everyone else on earth would be destroyed, but due to Noah's obedience and righteousness, he and his beloved family were called into safety. Noah and his wife, along with his sons and their wives, would enter the ark with the assurance of hope!

The Ark of Faith

And of every living thing of all flesh, you shall bring two of every kind into the ark, to keep them alive with you; they shall be male and female. Of the birds after their kind, and of the animals after their kind, of every creeping thing of the ground after its kind, two of every kind will come to you to keep them alive. As for you, take for yourself some of all food which is edible, and gather it to yourself; and it shall be for food for you and for them.

—Genesis 6:19–21

Besides His perplexing directive to build the ark, God had given Noah this specific, "crazy" command: Noah was to throw open the doors of the gargantuan boat so that two of every sort of animal, bird, and *creeping thing* could parade into the vessel! Now, if I had been in his shoes, I would have tried my best to obey God by building an unprecedented sailing vessel in the middle of the desert, but to open my new home to lions and tigers and bears? Oh my!

It has been my experience that God's commandments, although not burdensome, as John the apostle wrote in 1 John 5:3, will indeed stretch us out of our tiny zones of comfort. If you are accustomed to the pleasure of comfort, you are probably not going to enjoy the life God has called you to participate in! But if you long to leave a legacy that will stand for all of recorded time, then you must toss comfort aside and embrace the adventure and scope of God's fantastic story for your life.

You may not always understand God's instructions—but obey anyway! God's requests may seem absurd to your natural way of thinking—but obey anyway! God has never asked His children to fully understand, but He has simply asked us to follow Him. If we were to completely understand the reason for His instructions, there would be no need for faith. God has called each one of us who is experiencing a storm of epic proportions to trust Him even when nothing has been explained to us. Faith is our ark in all of life's storms.

Chased by the Blessing

Thus Noah did; according to all that God had commanded him, so he did. —Genesis 6:22

Oh, that God would say those exact words about me! Oh, that I would be known as a woman who immediately obeyed everything the Father commanded me to do. God will inevitably ask His children to do hard things, but when those hard things collide with the joy of obedience, you can be sure that the blessing of the Father will be following in close pursuit!

We often ignore the coming blessing and focus on the difficulty of obedience; time and time again, we forget about the joy and meditate on the mandate. The life of Noah is vibrant proof that the road to a lasting legacy is built upon a lifestyle of obedience and faithfulness.

It seems to me that because God's instructions were so specifically chronicled in the Bible, Noah's actual construction of the ark could have been detailed as well. The Holy Spirit and Moses, who wrote the book of Genesis, could have offered a blow-by-blow account of where Noah and his sons obtained the wood, the nails, the pitch, and the tar. The Bible could have stated clearly the steps it took to build a ship of that magnitude, but all the Bible says is this: *"Thus Noah did."* He did it! Noah obeyed God, and heaven applauded! In the New Testament book of Hebrews, we read,

---

By faith Noah, being warned by God about things not yet seen, in reverence prepared an ark for the salvation of his household, by which he condemned the world, and became an heir of the righteousness which is according to faith. —Hebrews 11:7

It has always amazed me that the Holy Spirit was still talking about the men and women of the Old Testament while writing the New Testament. Although Noah had lived thousands of years before Hebrews was written, the Holy Spirit was still so impressed by this man's life that He just had to mention it again! The memorable points concerning Noah's life that the Spirit references are his faith, his reverence, and his righteousness. Those are the same attributes the Holy Spirit values among God's people today. He is not impressed by our bank account, our retirement fund, the square footage of our home, our education, our looks, or any other external characteristic. What catches the attention of the Holy Spirit is our faith, our reverence, and our righteousness.

"Just as the wise sailor can use a head wind to carry him forward by tacking and taking advantage of its impelling force, so it is possible for us in our spiritual life through the victorious grace of God to turn to account the things that seem most unfriendly and unfavorable, and to be able to say continually, 'The things that were against me have happened to the furtherance of the gospel.'"

—Author unknown

TEN

RSVP to God

The righteous Noah and his family had obeyed the voice of the Lord; they had spent one hundred and twenty of the best years of their lives building an enormous boat that others mocked. After choosing to live uprightly in the midst of a culture of compromise, and after hearing the voice of the Lord and obeying it exactly, Noah was now called to yet another level of obedience.

God's Favorite Word

> Then the LORD said to Noah, "Come into the ark, you and all your household, because I have seen that you are righteous before Me in this generation." —Genesis 7:1 NKJV

In the days leading up to the tempest that would destroy every living thing on earth that was outside of the ark, God made this invitation to

Noah and his family: *"Come...."* Allow this word to usher your heart into a place of peace today. Regardless of what storm you may be facing, the Father is quietly but confidently asking you to come to Him; He is inviting you into the ark of His presence, where there is always safety and protection from any of life's storms. As a child of the living God, what destroys the lives of others will have no damaging power in yours when you respond to His glorious invitation to *"come."*

My heart breaks for those who are experiencing the ravaging forces of a storm today but have not responded to the hospitality and warmth of our loving God. I can't imagine any safer or more peaceful place in which to endure a storm than in the ark of His presence.

I have often thought that *come* must be one of God's favorite words—especially when talking with His dear children. He is always in pursuit of us, asking us to come to Him and enjoy His friendship. Noah was not the first person, nor was he the last, whom God has invited to "come" into friendship with Him. Here are some examples.

God invited Moses to come up on the mountain so he could hear God's voice and experience His presence:

> At that time the LORD said to me, "Cut out for yourself two tablets of stone like the former ones, and come up to Me on the mountain, and make an ark of wood for yourself."   —Deuteronomy 10:1

God invited the Israelites to seek Him, and the invitation still stands today:

> But you shall seek the LORD at the place which the LORD your God will choose from all your tribes, to establish His name there for His dwelling, and there you shall come.   —Deuteronomy 12:5

In the Psalms, time after time, through His servants, God invites His people to come:

Come, you children, listen to me; I will teach you the fear of the
LORD. —Psalm 34:11

Come and see the works of God, who is awesome in His deeds
toward the sons of men. —Psalm 66:5

Come and hear, all who fear God, and I will tell of what He has
done for my soul. —Psalm 66:16

Come, let us worship and bow down, let us kneel before the LORD
our Maker. —Psalm 95:6

Jesus Himself gave the invitation, to anyone who would listen, to simply come:

Come to Me, all who are weary and heavy-laden, and I will give
you rest. —Matthew 11:28

The call to come to Jesus includes the invitation to speak with Him and to be changed:

"Come now, and let us reason together," says the LORD, "though
your sins are as scarlet, they will be as white as snow; though they
are red like crimson, they will be like wool." —Isaiah 1:18

In the final chapter of the Bible, the Spirit and Jesus are still asking those created in the image of God to come to Him:

The Spirit and the bride say, "Come." And let the one who hears say, "Come." And let the one who is thirsty come; let the one who wishes take the water of life without cost. —Revelation 22:17

This is an invitation to which you must respond—you must not ignore the summons of God. In my life, I have found that this is an offer that deserves multiple acknowledgements in many situations. Yes, I have accepted Jesus as my Lord and Savior, and that is where it all begins. However, I must also accept His invitation into the ark of His presence during the stormiest days of my life. I can remain outside that presence and subject myself to the elements of worry, fear, anxiety, and even anger. Or, I can accept His invitation and experience the umbrella of His protection.

As you know by now, I have been deeply impacted theologically by the hymns that were introduced to me from the time I was a little girl, sitting on wooden church pews, swinging my lively feet, which were bedecked with white ruffled socks and black patent leather shoes. Often, when the winds of circumstances are blowing around me and the torrential downpour of difficult people is impeding my progress in life, I will sing to myself. No one hears the melody of my song except for Jesus and me. In such moments, I am responding to His *"Come."* In those quiet times, far away from stress and anxiety, I sing songs like this:

> Softly and tenderly Jesus is calling,
> Calling for you and for me;
> See, on the portals He's waiting and watching,
> Watching for you and for me.
>
> [Refrain:]
> Come home, come home,
> Ye who are weary, come home;
> Earnestly, tenderly, Jesus is calling,
> Calling, "O sinner, come home!"

. . . .

O for the wonderful love He has promised,
Promised for you and for me!
Though we have sinned, He has mercy and pardon,
Pardon for you and for me.

[Refrain:]
Come home, come home,
Ye who are weary, come home;
Earnestly, tenderly, Jesus is calling,
Calling, "O sinner, come home!"

A Sacred, Sailing Zoo

You shall take with you of every clean animal by sevens, a male and his female; and of the animals that are not clean two, a male and his female; also of the birds of the sky, by sevens, male and female, to keep offspring alive on the face of all the earth. For after seven more days, I will send rain on the earth forty days and forty nights; and I will blot out from the face of the land every living thing that I have made. Noah did according to all that the LORD had commanded him. —Genesis 7:2–5

Noah's immediate obedience to God's mandate concerning the inclusion of the animals humbles me when I think about all the times I have argued with God about things He has asked me to do. I can remember instance after instance when I have futilely tried to talk God either out of something or into something. I want to bow my head in utter shame as I recall the times when I have pridefully and presumptuously believed I knew better than God did. In contrast, as he had all along, Noah instantly obeyed what the Lord commanded him, even though it must have seemed absurd to him.

As a mother of five, I wear an invisible badge that testifies to the fact that during my child-rearing years, I exhibited a massive amount of organization skills, creativity, and humor. When Craig and I were raising the incredibly strong-willed and opinionated children that God had seen fit to give us, I was often known to say in a firm but controlled voice, "Delayed obedience is disobedience!" I wanted my children to know the importance of obeying right away—and all the way. I believe that I need to remind myself to practice what I preached to my children! Through the life of Noah, God is reminding each of us that delayed obedience is actually wanton disobedience.

People who live in a region that is about to be attacked by a monster storm must not wait until the rain begins to fall, the wind begins to roar, or the sky begins to darken before they board up windows, buy sandbags, or stock up on supplies. When the storm begins to hit, it is too late to prepare. So it is with our lives. If you wait to prepare for a storm when you have the alarming doctor's report in your hands or when you receive the emergency call in the middle of the night, your life will be quickly swamped and decimated by the effects of the storm.

However, if, like Noah, you determine to prepare for the deluge during days of sunshine and tranquility, your life will be ready for any tempest that dares come your way. What has God already called you to do in order to prepare for a storm that may be brewing on the horizon of your life even now? Let me offer some suggestions: God has called His people to tithe even when they think they can't afford it. God has called us to forgive those who have wronged us even if we think they don't deserve it. God has called us to regularly read the Word even when we don't believe we have time for it. God has called us to worship Him even when we don't feel like it.

The Lord is an expert at storm preparation, and it is vital that we obey His instructions without delay. Although it might have seemed preposterous to Noah and everyone around him to summon thousands of animals to join him on the ark, Noah did so with no sarcastic backtalk to the Lord, the One who knows best! Once again, I have to say, "Oh, how I long to be like Noah!" I long to be a woman at my moment in history who doesn't ever question God, who refuses to argue with Him but follows through immediately!

Choosing to obey the Lord during the peaceful times in life can become a sacred act of submission on our part. When we obey, our ark will be fully stocked for the upcoming period of unstable circumstances and will remain a place of peaceful refuge from the furor happening around us.

Where Did They All Come From?

Now Noah was six hundred years old when the flood of water came upon the earth. Then Noah and his sons and his wife and his sons' wives with him entered the ark because of the water of the flood. Of clean animals and animals that are not clean and birds and everything that creeps on the ground, there went into the ark to Noah by twos, male and female, as God had commanded Noah. It came about after the seven days, that the water of the flood came upon the earth. —Genesis 7:6–10

Don't miss the miracle that happened before the storm! Noah had obeyed the voice of God, had built the massive ark, had invited his wife, his sons, and his sons' wives to join him, and then simply opened the doors for the animals to come in. The Bible doesn't recount a massive roundup of creatures large and small; it doesn't tell a story of Noah and his sons forcing the animals into the boat. It simply says that the animals went into the ark.

Isn't it interesting that the animals knew instinctively that a storm was about to hit the earth? Isn't it jaw-dropping to realize that the animals responded to the unction of God?

I find it equally intriguing that although the doors of the ark remained opened for the seven days before the flood started, no other people asked to go inside. Animals willingly responded and went inside, but the people stayed outside. Animals answered the invitation of God, but the people refused to join Noah and his family to secure a place of divine safety and protection. Bible teacher J. Vernon McGee said, "For seven days the world could have knocked at the door of the ark, and frankly, they could have come in—God would have saved them. All they had to do was to believe God."[3]

Not much has changed in the nearly five thousand years since the ark was built by Noah, has it? People are still ignoring or rejecting the sweet invitation of God to *"come."* Yet still He invites us and yearns for the door of our hearts to open to Him:

Behold, I stand at the door and knock; if anyone hears My voice and opens the door, I will come in to him and will dine with him, and he with Me. —Revelation 3:20

One Final Call

In the six hundredth year of Noah's life, in the second month, on the seventeenth day of the month, on the same day all the fountains of the great deep burst open, and the floodgates of the sky were opened. The rain fell upon the earth for forty days and forty nights. On the very same day Noah and Shem and Ham and Japheth, the sons of Noah, and Noah's wife and the three wives of his sons with them, entered the ark. —Genesis 7:11–13

The Bible records the remarkable fact that not only did it rain from the skies, but also the *"fountains"* from deep below the surface of the earth opened up and multiplied the amount of water in the flood.

According to these verses, the family of Noah seems to have entered the ark on the very day the waters were unleashed by heaven. This indicates they were still outside the ark for the last seven days beforehand

3. J. Vernon McGee, *Genesis Chapters 1–15*, Thru the Bible Commentary Series: The Law (Nashville, TN: Thomas Nelson, 1995), https://books.google.com/books?id=1NjsPcNIHIAC&pg=PT132&lpg=PT132&dq=For+seven+days+the+world+could+have+knocked+at+the+door+of+the+Ark.

(see Genesis 7:10), even though it had been completed and was ready to float upon the waters. I wonder what they were doing during those days. Perhaps they spent that time reaching out to other loved ones or acquaintances, imploring them to come with them on the ark. We can only imagine what might have transpired, but perhaps God, through the family of Noah, was giving people one final opportunity to turn away from their sin and turn toward the invitation of God Almighty.

As I ponder these possibilities, I know I need to examine my own life and what I do with the time I have been given. I must use every day to join my voice with the voice of God and invite the people of my generation to "*come.*" I must not be intimidated, embarrassed, or afraid to share with my generation the truth of the message of Jesus. This, my friend, is also part of the preparation for the storms that might lie ahead of us. It is strikingly clear that we are living in a moment in history when people have a desperate need for Jesus. We must invite our world into the protection of the presence of Jesus before it is too late. We simply must.

I often say that I live to "make hell smaller and heaven bigger." It is the clarion call from my Creator, to which I have responded with every breath I breathe, every ounce of energy I possess, and every bit of talent I have been given. Preparation for the storms of life is not just about protecting oneself; it is always, and forever will be, also about preparing those who have never heard of the Shelter in which they can take refuge.

God Closed the Door

Every beast after its kind, and all the cattle after their kind, and every creeping thing that creeps on the earth after its kind, and every bird after its kind, all sort of birds...went into the ark to Noah, by twos of all flesh in which was the breath of life. Those that entered, male and female of all flesh, entered as God had commanded him; and the Lord closed it behind him.

—Genesis 7:14–16

Don't you just love this one last detail of the grand parade of animal and bird life that joined Noah and his family in the ark? This is a miraculous, quiet detail that you might miss if you read this final piece of information too quickly. The *New Living Translation* renders the last part of the above passage as, *"Then the LORD closed the door behind them,"* while the *New International Version* states succinctly and with little emotion, *"Then the LORD shut him in."*

Noah didn't have to decide when to close the great, wooden door because God closed it at just the right moment in order to protect His precious crew of people and creatures. Likewise, we can be sure that when a storm is on the horizon of our lives, God will enact the security maneuver at just the right moment. When we have obeyed Him and wrapped ourselves in His righteousness, He will do what He alone can do: He will close the protective door in order to preserve us—for our sake and for the sake of generations to come.

God Wept

Then the flood came upon the earth for forty days, and the water increased and lifted up the ark, so that it rose above the earth. The water prevailed and increased greatly upon the earth, and the ark floated on the surface of the water. The water prevailed more and more upon the earth, so that all the high mountains everywhere under the heavens were covered. The water prevailed fifteen cubits higher, and the mountains were covered. All flesh that moved on the earth perished, birds and cattle and beasts and every swarming thing that swarms upon the earth, and all mankind; of all that was on the dry land, all in whose nostrils was the breath of the spirit of life, died. Thus He blotted out every living thing that was upon the face of the land, from man to animals to creeping things and to birds of the sky, and they were blotted out from the earth; and only Noah was left, together with those that were with him in the ark. The water prevailed upon the earth one hundred and fifty days.

—Genesis 7:17–24

When human beings reject their Creator, there will always be a price to pay; there will inevitably be a death. God fulfilled what He had announced He would do a hundred and twenty years earlier. He had warned the people, but they had ignored His call and His admonition. It was as if the rains that fell on the earth for forty dark and prolonged days were the tears of God falling from heaven to earth. The Creator took no pleasure in wiping out men and women who had been made in His image; He wept as He heard their cries even as the waters rose.

This storm, from which Noah and his family were protected, was like the visible representation of the tumult in the heart of God over those whom He had created to enjoy intimate fellowship with Him. In the New Testament, Jesus similarly wept over the people of the city of Jerusalem:

Jerusalem, Jerusalem, who kills the prophets and stones those who are sent to her! How often I wanted to gather your children together, the way a hen gathers her chicks under her wings, and you were unwilling. Behold, your house is being left to you desolate! —Matthew 23:37–38

We serve a God who cares intensely about the souls of His children and the type of eternity they choose. Thus, in Noah's day, God wept over the immense sin of His creation. He grieved so deeply that it caused a flood of cataclysmic proportions on the earth.

"God often uses something external to bring the Church to her knees. We ought to see it as the kindness of God when He allows trouble to drive us to prayer."

—R. T. Kendall

ELEVEN

God Remembered

But God remembered Noah and all the beasts and all the cattle that were with him in the ark; and God caused a wind to pass over the earth, and the water subsided. Also the fountains of the deep and the floodgates of the sky were closed, and the rain from the sky was restrained; and the water receded steadily from the earth, and at the end of one hundred and fifty days the water decreased. In the seventh month, on the seventeenth day of the month, the ark rested upon the mountains of Ararat. The water decreased steadily until the tenth month; in the tenth month, on the first day of the month, the tops of the mountains became visible.

—Genesis 8:1–5

The flood was finally over and the waters were at last beginning to recede from the face of the earth. Noah and his family had been protected from the torrential rains that had beat upon the roof of the ark and the massive floodwaters that had risen to cover even the tops of the mountains.

I can hardly keep from weeping as I read the first four words of this chapter of new beginnings: *"But God remembered Noah."* What reassurance is found in that quartet of words! How they describe the heart of God toward His people! God never forgets even one of His own, which means that you, my friend, are not forgotten, no matter how vicious the storm that has ravaged your life. You have been on God's mind throughout the entire ordeal, and there will come a moment when the floodwaters of your storm will begin to subside in the light of His grace.

Open the Windows of Your Heart

After spending well over 350 stuffy, endless days in the ark with lions and hyenas and magpies, Noah and his family were nearly free to begin living on dry ground once again. I can just imagine their delight, can't you? As the tossing of the ark upon the violent floodwaters gradually became a gentle rocking motion as the waters calmed, and then as the righteous passengers felt the ark jolt to a stop upon some type of ground, I wonder if a cheer went up from within the sailing vessel! I can only suppose that the women began to weep for joy, knowing that their days within the dark and damp floating zoo were about over. Surely, there was no sweeter moment in Mrs. Noah's life than the moment that was recounted in Scripture with these words: *"and the water subsided"* (Genesis 8:1). Finally, she would be free of the smell of manure and the bad breath of donkeys. Finally, she would be able to plant a garden and hang her laundry out to dry. At long last, the storm was over and she would be free to live again.

No storm lasts forever—even though it might feel as if your particular storm has been never-ending. If you are weary due to the length of the deluge that has poured into your life, look for signs of a new beginning. Listen for the sounds of a peaceful new day. Observe what is going on around you and begin to expect to experience the cessation of that which has rocked your life and your world.

As you become aware of the closing chapter of your storm, take time to rejoice in all that God has done for you in the midst of it. Don't miss the opportunity to gulp in the fresh air of the new beginning God has provided just for you. Plan what you will do now that the tempest is past and find delight in the world you have been given. Don't allow what the storm has ravaged to define your life in this new season. Move beyond the despair, the discouragement, and the darkness and open your heart and life to the new day God has prepared for you.

Peace At Last!

Then it came about at the end of forty days, that Noah opened the window of the ark which he had made; and he sent out a raven, and it flew here and there until the water was dried up from the earth. Then he sent out a dove from him, to see if the water was abated from the face of the land; but the dove found no resting place for the sole of her foot, so she returned to him into the ark, for the water was on the surface of all the earth. Then he put out his hand and took her and brought her into the ark himself. So he waited yet another seven days; and again he sent out the dove from the ark. The dove came to him toward evening, and behold, in her beak was a freshly picked olive leaf. So Noah knew that the water was abated from the earth. Then he waited yet another seven days, and sent out the dove; but she did not return to him again.

—Genesis 8:6–12

Even though, for quite some time, Noah's family had sensed that the flood was finally over, it was when the sweet dove returned to the ark with an olive branch in its beak that they knew for certain the storm had indeed ended.

There are some details in the above passage that are so dear, so intimate, and so amazing that my heart leaps within me when I read them and I can barely keep from weeping. Noah sent out a nondescript dove to discern whether it was safe to leave the ark. This dove, one of the most humble of God's created species, came back with an olive branch in her small mouth. An olive branch is a sign of peace. The war was over and God was declaring His peace upon all of creation.

God has extended His olive branch to us in the form of His Son Jesus. Will you accept the peace offering He is giving to you as your storm passes by? Will you recognize the hand and power of God in your life and begin to live again with joy and delight? I enthusiastically invite you to throw open the window of your heart and embrace the new season that inevitably comes after a storm. Don't remain in the deluge of the past but determine today that God is with you in this peaceful new season and it is time for you to dream again. So many people allow the storm to linger beyond the days of its impact, but you can choose to imitate the example of Noah and thrown open the window of your life. You can expect to see God's goodness all around you.

It's Finally Time!

Now it came about in the six hundred and first year, in the first month, on the first of the month, the water was dried up from the earth. Then Noah removed the covering of the ark, and looked, and behold, the surface of the ground was dried up. In the second month, on the twenty-seventh day of the month, the earth was dry. Then God spoke to Noah, saying, "Go out of the ark, you and your wife and your sons and your sons' wives with you. Bring out with you every living thing of all flesh that is with you, birds and animals and every creeping thing that creeps on the earth, that they may breed abundantly on the earth, and be fruitful and multiply on the earth." So Noah went out, and his sons and his wife and his sons' wives with him. Every beast, every creeping thing, and every bird, everything that moves on the earth, went out by their families from the ark. —Genesis 8:13–19

I am not particularly fond of waiting, are you? Yet I have determined that waiting is unavoidable. I wait in doctor's offices, I wait at stoplights, I wait for my kids to call me, and I wait for winter to pass. I wait in long lines at the grocery store. I wait on the telephone when I am put on hold by the technical services department of a company from which I am seeking help about some electronic gadget whose use escapes my mental expertise. We all must wait for something, so we might as well decide to *wait well.*

Waiting well encompasses numerous disciplines that can be embraced even when it seems we are at the end of our patience—or even our rope. For example, I often coach single women to wait well for their future spouses; they can wait well by serving the Lord wholeheartedly and developing into the godly women He created them to be. For them, part of waiting well might include teaching Sunday school or going on a missions trip.

Single women should know that married women often need to wait too. When a young wife is dealing with anxiety because she has not yet conceived a child, she might consider working in the church nursery, offering to babysit for her friends, or even becoming a foster parent while she waits to hold a child of her own, whether by adoption or by birth. There are many things to wait for. As a very young grandmother who lives thousands of miles away from her grandchildren, I have developed sweet relationships with the children at my church and in my neighborhood as I wait for the next time I can embrace those sweet faces that carry my genes.

The wait Noah and his family experienced before they could leave the ark must have seemed unending to them, and yet they stayed inside the vessel until God said, *"Go out of the ark."* Waiting for the timing of God is often one of the most difficult parts of a storm that assails our lives. However, you can be sure that God will speak to you at just the right time and give you instructions about your "new beginnings party"!

We don't know what Noah and his family did while they waited, but we do know that *they did, indeed, wait* until God said, "Now!" They waited in uncomfortable conditions—in the putrid odor of the massive menagerie—until God said it was time for them to leave. If they had left too early, it could have been disastrous! You will avoid disaster, too, if you can simply and patiently wait for God to declare, "Now is the time." Everything He is preparing for you is worth the wait He requires of you.

Great Is Thy Faithfulness

Then Noah built an altar to the Lord, and took of every clean animal and of every clean bird and offered burnt offerings on the altar. The Lord smelled the soothing aroma, and the Lord said to Himself, "I will never again curse the ground on account of man, for the intent of man's heart is evil from his youth; and I will never again destroy every living thing as I have done. While the earth remains, seedtime and harvest, and cold and heat, and summer and winter, and day and night shall not cease."

—Genesis 8:20–22

The very first action that Noah chose to take after disembarking from the ark was to build an altar to the Lord! God remembered Noah, and Noah remembered the Lord! Noah didn't bemoan the fact that he had no house to live in or complain about the lack of cultivated fields; he expressed his gratitude to the God who makes all things new. He worshipped the Lord before he romped on the dry land, built a home, or tilled the ground. Even though the entire world stretched out before him, he took the time to thank God for His protection and provision.

Then, as Noah offered his first sacrifice to the Lord since the deluge, God caught the scent of something beautiful! The Lord loved the fragrance of the aroma that was wafting toward heaven at that moment. God's sense of smell was in an exuberant state as He experienced the worship of Noah.

As you exit your storm, if you want to make God happy, choose to worship Him. If you long to delight the heart of God, offer Him a sacrifice of praise. Take some focused time just to thank Him for His guidance and wisdom. Remind yourself that although your situation might have been fearful and distressing, God was with you every step of the way.

Remember that when our lives have been plundered by an unremitting storm, we often don't "feel" like worshipping, but that is when we should worship the longest and the loudest! When the storm has been devastating and you have experienced crop failure of enormous proportions, that is when you should lift your hands and declare, *"I will bless the LORD at all times; His praise shall continually be in my mouth"* (Psalm 34:1)!

The Postscript of God

And God blessed Noah and his sons and said to them, "Be fruitful and multiply, and fill the earth.... As for you, be fruitful and multiply; populate the earth abundantly and multiply in it."

—Genesis 9:1, 7

The God of creation, who had wept over the sin of humanity and who had closed the door of the ark, now blessed Noah, his sons, and their wives! It was a time, once again, as it had been in the garden of Eden, when He was delighted with His creation. The storm had passed by and new life had begun in its fullness and abundance. What a glorious day for Noah and his family! They were now experiencing in a new way the shining grace and favor of God Almighty.

My prayer for you, in the aftermath of your storm, is that you will feel the pleasure of God on your life. I pray that you will know His favor and blessing upon you as you begin to rebuild what the storm has taken from you. If you are still dealing with the trauma that the storm has afflicted and are unable to escape the effects of having been pillaged by the tempest, perhaps you could gather the courage to pray this prayer:

Lord, would You now bless me as You blessed Noah and his family? Would You fill me with Your abundant life? I come to You humbly and ask You to smile upon me and help me to begin again. Amen.

God Keeps Every Promise He Makes

Then God spoke to Noah and to his sons with him, saying, "Now behold, I Myself do establish My covenant with you, and with your descendants after you.... I establish My covenant with you; and all flesh shall never again be cut off by the water of the flood, neither shall there again be a flood to destroy the earth." God said, "This is the sign of the covenant which I am making between Me and you and every living creature that is with you, for all successive generations; I set My bow in the cloud, and it shall be for a sign of a covenant between Me and the earth. It shall come about, when I bring a cloud over the earth, that the bow will be seen in the cloud, and I will remember My covenant, which is between Me and you and every living creature of all flesh; and never again shall the water become a flood to destroy all flesh. When the bow is in the cloud, then I will look upon it, to remember the everlasting covenant between God and every living creature of all flesh that is on the earth." —Genesis 9:8–9, 11–16

We serve a covenant-making and promise-keeping God! As you leave behind the havoc that a storm has created in your life, remember that God keeps every promise He makes. He is a faithful God who is true to His Word. He will always have the last word, and it will always be a good word! We may never completely know the purpose of the storm we go through, but we can know that God always keep His promises.

In the Noahic Covenant, God gave an unconditional, no-strings-attached promise that He would never again destroy the earth with a flood. As the years went by, I can imagine that as they experienced various degrees of rain showers, Noah and his family had to remind themselves to stay in a place of faith and trust that the Father was not sending another flood. Although it would rain again, they knew that the God who had made the promise would be faithful to keep that promise.

And then, as the great "Amen" to the flood, God gave a visual demonstration whose sign would serve as a reminder in all the ages to come that He had made a commitment never again to destroy creation with a deluge. The visual demonstration of God's eternal promise was a rainbow.

In Genesis 9, the Hebrew word that is translated *"bow"* is *qesheth*, and it was generally used as the description of the bow of a warrior. It was the bow that archers would use for hunting and soldiers would use in battle. Perhaps what God was assuring Noah and his family that sunny day was that He had hung up His bow; the judgment on humanity has ceased. What a beautiful promise! What an awesome God!

"In the secret of God's tabernacle no enemy can find us
and no troubles can reach us. The pride of man and the
strife of tongues find no entrance into the pavilion of God.
The secret of His presence is a more secure refuge than a
thousand Gibraltars. I do not mean that no trials come. They
may come in abundance but they cannot penetrate into the
sanctuary of the soul, and we may dwell in perfect peace even
in the midst of life's fiercest storms."

—Hannah Whitall Smith

PART FOUR

Mea Culpa!

TWELVE

What Were You Thinking?

Is it possible to run away from God? What happens when we try? These are just two of the questions we will explore while reviewing a little book that tells a *big* storm story! The book of Jonah is nestled among the Minor Prophets in the last part of the Old Testament. This book is only four chapters long, but its riveting theme has the power the leave eternal footprints on our hearts today.

Demonstrating the Heart of God

> *The word of the LORD came to Jonah the son of Amittai saying, "Arise, go to Nineveh the great city and cry against it, for their wickedness has come up before Me."* —Jonah 1:1–2

God spoke to the prophet Jonah out of His rich wisdom, His consummate holiness, and His tender compassion. His words were directional, commanding Jonah to go to the city of Nineveh and speak up for righteousness. Nineveh was an evil city whose people were involved in wretched sin. Worship of the true God was nowhere to be found in that perverse place, so the Lord decided to send His servant Jonah there to have a man on the scene who would speak up for righteousness and call the people to repent.

God needed just one person who would be His voice to that wicked and reprobate culture. This is what God is asking of each of us as well—He needs His children to speak His words and demonstrate His heart to the culture in which they live. Sometimes, as He did with Jonah, He will speak directly to one of His servants with specific instructions regarding this commission.

The Super Bowl and Nineveh

A few years ago, Craig and I invited our church staff to our home to enjoy that annual American experience known as "The Super Bowl." None of us really had a team in the game that we were passionate about. We just couldn't wait to enjoy the music, the commercials, and the celebration. Oh, and the food! We looked forward to eating our way through the entire game!

Now, let me just admit that whenever I watch one of my favorite TV series, I often "DVR" it so I can fast forward through the commercials. I am not sure I have ever purchased a single item due to viewing a TV commercial made by some advertising agency that only wants my money. Commercials, in general, are a waste of time for this all-American girl. (Except, maybe, for food commercials. They are definitely not a waste of time!)

However, traditionally, whenever I have watched the Super Bowl, all the commercials have drawn me in. The commercials are as fascinating to me as the game itself! This particular year, some of the commercials were funny, some were entertaining, and some told a sweet story. Yet we soon began to notice that many of the commercials were suggestive and provocative, and some were vile and inappropriate. While watching the biggest game of America's favorite pastime, we all had to turn our heads and our hearts away from the TV screen during the commercial breaks. At one point, our worship leader, Kelly, and I got up and walked into the kitchen, away from the commercials. We weren't even hungry anymore—we had lost our appetites.

Kelly often comes to me with questions of the heart, and she looked at me over a Crock-Pot of my famous Chicken Wing Dip and said, "Carol, how did we come to this? Why are commercials now pornographic?"

The kitchen was filled with others who had also walked away from the immoral advertising on the TV screen, but no one was able to answer Kelly's question. We were all sober and silent. Eventually, I stirred up some humility and courage and responded, "Kelly, I think it is because of me. I have not spoken up in America. Christians have not infiltrated ad agencies and the entertainment industry. I think it is because no one is speaking God's voice to those worlds."

In that moment, we muted the football game that was being watched in millions of homes around the world and prayed for America. We prayed fervently that God would send His messengers to the entertainment culture and to the advertising world.

A Dude Named Jonah

If you have ever spent even a half hour in a Sunday school classroom, you most likely know what happens next in the story of this dude named Jonah:

But Jonah rose up to flee to Tarshish from the presence of the Lord. So he went down to Joppa, found a ship which was going to Tarshish, paid the fare and went down into it to go with them to Tarshish from the presence of the Lord. —Jonah 1:3

Jonah actually turned God down!

Jonah…Jonah…Jonah…what were you thinking? Didn't you know that it is definitely not possible to run away from God? Oh, Jonah…didn't you know that God's ways are always the very best?

Although we might want to ask Jonah those very valid questions, the truth is, perhaps it is time for all of us to do some self-examination. Rather than aim those searching questions at a man from Bible history, maybe we should interview ourselves, asking, "Self, didn't you know that it is not possible to run away from God? Me, myself, and I, don't you realize that God's ways are always the best?"

Jonah apparently didn't think about or pray about his answer to God—he just said an unequivocal and defiant, "No!" Then he ran away as hard and as fast as he could! This prophet definitely did not show God the respect that Moses did when he was asked to do something difficult for the Lord. At least Moses responded with, "Are you sure, God? Are you sure that it is me whom You want?" (See Exodus 3:1–4:17.)

I can assure you that God is still speaking today. He has an enormous amount of work for His servants to accomplish during their time in human history. In case you haven't noticed it lately, the world is still a place of sin and compromise, and our God is still a righteous and holy God.

In Jonah's day, not only was Nineveh a heathen city, but the Israelites considered its people, the Assyrians, to be archenemies of the people of God. Israel had been tormented by this city. The Assyrians were well-known for the intimidation and torture techniques they used on their enemies. No wonder Jonah didn't want to go to Nineveh!

Has the Lord ever asked you to do something so difficult that it has caused you to have dry mouth, knocking knees, and a bad case of circumstance-induced nausea? If you would lay down your defenses for just a minute and let me give you a tip, it would be this: when God offers you a job, no matter how hard it is—don't turn Him down! Say yes to the Lord no matter how outrageous the request may seem to you, no matter how loud your knees are knocking, and no matter how fast your heart is beating.

I have always thought it quite interesting that God offered Jonah a job that He knew His prophet was going to turn down. God was not surprised by Jonah's response because He understood, even before He offered the commission, that Jonah would make a mad dash for Tarshish. It's also quite interesting that God knows even before He speaks to us what our response will be—and yet He still speaks.

God continues to call people whom He knows will run away from His voice and His purposes. He speaks because He is a loving pursuer and He isn't one to throw His hands up in frustration over one of His beloved children. Our heavenly Father has never been known to say, "There's another one who won't listen! Why do I get all the wimps?" When we refuse to obey, God waits, and then He will speak to us again. When we run in the other direction, He is patient, but He will never stop pursuing those who are His own.

God will perpetually pursue you—sometimes by using a storm—just as He did Jonah. He will pursue you with His love, His goodness, and His voice of direction.

I will make an everlasting covenant with them, that I will not turn away from following them, to do them good.
—Jeremiah 32:40 ASV

God's love and goodness are chasing you down, regardless of how you have responded to His call!

Surely goodness and lovingkindness will follow me all the days of my life.
—Psalm 23:6

An Exorbitant Cost!

Jonah had to pay the fare before he was allowed to board the ship that was headed to Tarshish. My friend, there is always a high price to pay for saying no to the Father. There is a price to pay for running away from God. There is a price to pay for disagreeing with the Word and for leaving God's almighty and loving presence. It is a price that you can't afford, and it will put you in "debt" for a long, long time. The price that is required of you might just cost you your abundant life! Life is always less abundant when you run away from God because any hope of living abundantly is found where He is! Joy is found in His presence and peace is discovered when you choose to trust Him.

In Your presence is fullness of joy. —Psalm 16:11

The steadfast of mind You will keep in perfect peace because he trusts in You. —Isaiah 26:3

Knowing that the price of fleeing from God's presence and ignoring His instructions is much too high, why would anyone choose to run away from the Lord and ignore His wisdom? Who, in their right mind, would turn God down? Unfortunately, as part of the self-examination that this chapter requires, we must admit that most of us do this—frequently. We do it so often and so callously that turning away from God has become a sad ritual, almost an obnoxious discipline. Too many times to count, I have smugly thought I had a better idea for living my life than God has. Whenever you or I violate God's Word and promote our own desires, we are turning God down and running away from His loving presence.

The good news is that you can run, my friend, but you just can't hide! It is impossible for you to actually leave the presence of God, no matter how strong your rebellion might be:

Where can I go from Your Spirit? Or where can I flee from Your presence? If I ascend to heaven, You are there; if I make my bed in Sheol, behold, You are there. If I take the wings of the dawn, if I dwell in the remotest part of the sea, even there Your hand will lead me, and Your right hand will lay hold of me.

—Psalm 139:7–10

For I am convinced that neither death, nor life, nor angels, nor principalities, nor things present, nor things to come, nor powers,

*nor height, nor depth, nor any other created thing, will be able
to separate us from the love of God, which is in Christ Jesus our
Lord.* —Romans 8:38–39

Take it from Jonah (and from me), you can say no to God, but you will
never escape His goodness or His presence. One of the many things the
Father does best is to pursue His obstinate children.

Self-Inflicted Storms

*The LORD hurled a great wind on the sea and there was a great
storm on the sea so that the ship was about to break up.*

—Jonah 1:4

Often, the price we pay for attempting to run away from the voice and
presence of the Lord can be described as a "self-inflicted storm." In our
mistrust of the Father and in our rebellion, we can foolishly bring horrific
circumstances and unbearable events upon ourselves. Not all storms in life
are stirred up by selfishness and pride, but many are. We create the right
conditions for storm-tossed living when we make the decision, like Jonah
did, to turn God down.

For instance, when a young couple decides to engage in premarital sex
and the woman becomes pregnant, they have to deal with their choice to
act in a way that is contrary to God's Word—and with the storm it has
created. I am not implying that a baby is a "storm," because all babies are
precious and are blessings; however, the young people may have to deal
with the challenges of single parenting, the pain of giving a child up for
adoption, or the change in direction their life has now taken.

Or, when a person chooses to overspend and live above their income
level, they can create a storm that includes indebtedness, the invasion of
constant phone calls from creditors, and an inability to save and give to
God's work.

When someone chooses to embrace a lifestyle that leads to alcohol or drug addiction, it can stir up appalling conditions. Tragic accidents, the loss of a job, homelessness, or a lack of identity and direction can all be elements of a storm system caused by such a choice.

Have your choices created unfavorable atmospheric conditions, causing a storm to brew on the horizon of your life? I have discovered that there are enough other types of storms in my life for me to endure without giving sin the power to stir up extra and monstrous blasts!

Then the sailors became afraid and every man cried to his god, and they threw the cargo which was in the ship into the sea to lighten it for them. But Jonah had gone below into the hold of the ship, lain down and fallen sound asleep. —Jonah 1:5

Jonah's decision to run away from God impacted not only his life, but also the life of every other person who was on the high-priced yacht on which he was traveling. We need to consider how this type of consequence applies to our own lives. Your self-inflicted storm will invariably affect the lives of those around you. You might mistakenly think, *My choices are nobody else's business,* but none of us, my friend, is an island. Our family members, our coworkers, and our friends are often greatly impacted by the ripples caused by our daily choices.

It is clear that when you sin and then choose to run from God, the people around you will pay the price as well. When you choose fear over faith, and self over sacrifice, the waves of your storm can violently splash upon the people whom you love dearly.

So the captain approached [Jonah] and said, "How is it that you are sleeping? Get up, call on your god. Perhaps your god will be concerned about us so that we will not perish." Each man said to his mate, "Come, let us cast lots so we may learn on whose account this calamity has struck us." So they cast lots and the lot fell on Jonah. Then they said to him, "Tell us, now! On whose account has this calamity struck us? What is your occupation? And where do you come from? What is your country? From what people are you?" He said to them, "I am a Hebrew, and I fear the LORD God of heaven who made the sea and the dry land." Then the men became extremely frightened and they said to him, "How could you do this?" For the men knew that he was fleeing from the presence of the LORD, because he had told them. So they said to him, "What should we do to you that the sea may become calm for us?"—for the sea was becoming increasingly stormy. He said to them, "Pick me up and throw me into the sea. Then the sea will become calm for you, for I know that on account of me this great storm has come upon you."

—Jonah 1:6–12

When Jonah was awakened from his slumber and confronted by his poor choices, he had the wisdom to admit that the storm was his fault. He confessed to the alarmed captain and crew of the ship that they had nothing to do with this storm—it was his fault, and his fault alone.

Taking the blame for the atrocious storm was the first step in the right direction for the errant Jonah. The blustery winds and stormy waves would have continued for the entire trip if Jonah had not taken responsibility for those wretched conditions.

Is there something in your life that you need to take responsibility for? Is there a sin that you have been hiding and even ignoring? Are you "sleeping" while others pay for the price for your reckless choices? The first step toward a peaceful life is to repent and take the blame. If Jonah could do it—so can you.

Overboard!

However, the men rowed desperately to return to land but they could not, for the sea was becoming even stormier against them. Then they called on the LORD and said, "We earnestly pray, O LORD, do not let us perish on account of this man's life and do not put innocent blood on us; for You, O LORD, have done as You have pleased." So they picked up Jonah, threw him into the sea, and the sea stopped its raging. —Jonah 1:13–15

The sailors hadn't wanted to throw Jonah overboard to certain death, so they tried to make it back to land instead; however, in the end, when they couldn't fight against the storm, they felt they were left with no choice.

Consider yourself forewarned by the story of Jonah! When you run from God's voice and ignore His calling, you are going to be in over your head! You are going to be in *way, way* over your head. You will land in a situation that you are unable to control, that you would never have chosen, and that threatens to overwhelm you.

I believe that the devil often endeavors to convince us to say no to God (or to have us mistakenly believe that God really doesn't speak to His children today). The enemy always tries to have us respond in fear and not in faith. I can just picture that dastardly devil rubbing his little hands together in glee because he has evilly connived to get us to run away from God rather than toward God. I can imagine that Old Slew Foot himself jumping up and down in delight when one of God's own children says, "No, Father! Not me! I'm not doing it!"

Satan wants you overboard in the storm in which you have found yourself; he wants you to sputter and panic and struggle for air as others watch you sink. Let me just reiterate this storm principle so that you never forget it: when you say no to God, you are going to be in over your head!

The Most Powerful Words

When Jonah took responsibility for his own sin and repented in front of other people who didn't know the Lord, it changed their lives for all of eternity. Jonah had been chosen by God to make a difference, and every word that he spoke and choice that he made mattered deeply to the world around him. Jonah's words and choices mattered very, very much. You, my friend, have been chosen by God to make a difference in the world in which you live. And just like Jonah, every word that you speak and every choice that you make matters to the world around you. It matters very, very much.

The world is waiting for a man or a woman to make the right choice and do the right thing. As a believer in Jesus Christ, when you have sinned or made a serious error in judgment, take responsibility for it. Sometimes the two most powerful words you can ever say are, "I'm sorry." Those two words, when coupled with a repentant heart, have the power to change the lives of those who are watching your life.

Then the men feared the LORD greatly, and they offered a sacrifice to the LORD and made vows. —Jonah 1:16

The men in Noah's boat changed their minds! They no longer looked to false gods for protection or for deliverance. Not only did they change their minds, but they also worshipped the true God on that storm-ravaged ship as the sea began to calm down.

In every storm, you have power! You have the power of repentance and the power of honesty. Remember that the strength of a storm always lessens when a person simply says, "I was wrong. I'm sorry."

However, for Jonah, the effects of the storm were not quite over. He was still overboard in the sea, and his journey was about to continue in a fantastic and horrific manner. Saying "I'm sorry" often does not recuse a person from the aftermath of the choices they have made, but it can lead them to a vital restored relationship with God. In Jonah's case, admitting his fault made a way for him to reconnect with the Lord God who had called him and empowered him.

And the LORD appointed a great fish to swallow Jonah, and Jonah was in the stomach of the fish three days and three nights. —Jonah 1:17

Jonah was in the midst of the adventure of his life! The prophet never could have imagined or dreamed of the impact that his time in the belly of a fish would have on people's lives for thousands of years. At this moment, all that Jonah saw were fish innards, floating seaweed, and undigested sea urchins. All that he could smell was refuse that had not yet been regurgitated, excrement that had not yet been eliminated, and sweat dripping from his own body. Jonah had no idea what was about to happen next—and neither do you in the midst of your own storm. But what Jonah believed was the very worst moment of his life was about to turn into a miracle. He did not yet understand that what he thought was a hideous sentence of death was about to become a wonderful deliverance!

"When you come out of the storm, you won't be the same person that walked in. That's what the storm is all about."

—Author unknown

THIRTEEN

An "Aha!" Moment

In every storm and in every bewildering environment of your life, God's chief desire is that you cry out to Him. When you find yourself in a place of terror and solitary confinement, God wants your attention. He simply wants to hear your voice amid the wind and the waves. He longs to be your ultimate comfort and safe shelter. And when you at least respond to the God of Jonah, you, too, will experience a divine "Aha!" moment that will change the trajectory of your life.

Spitting Out Seaweed

Then Jonah prayed to the LORD his God from the stomach of the fish, and he said, "I called out of my distress to the LORD, and He answered me. I cried for help from the depth of Sheol; You heard my voice. For You had cast me into the deep, into the heart of the seas, and the current engulfed me. All Your breakers and billows passed over me. So I said, 'I have been expelled from Your sight.

Nevertheless I will look again toward Your holy temple.'"

—Jonah 2:1–4

———————

Jonah had been about one gulp of salt water away from death when God rescued him. The waves had covered him and he was rapidly descending into the deepest and darkest part of the sea. There was no rescue boat on the way or safety net in sight—but God reached down from heaven, scooped Jonah up, and placed him safely in the belly of a very large fish!

Even when you have said that infamous and rebellious "No" to God, when you've paid a price you couldn't afford, when your sins have obnoxiously splashed all over the lives of others, and when you are in way over your head, God will rescue you! The Lord will never give up on one of His very own who has the humility and honesty to say, "I'm sorry, Father. It was my fault." At the very instant that Jonah uttered those unpretentious yet revealing words to God, the rescue began! Likewise, your rescue will begin when you follow Jonah's example and declare to God—and to others—"I'm sorry. It was my fault."

God is a pursuer, and He will track you down with creative resolve and unimaginable wit. As the storm was calming down, the sailors were worshipping, and Jonah was spitting out seaweed, I wonder if God looked over to the angel on His left and said, "You ain't seen nothin' yet!"

The truth is that God will, indeed, rescue you—but the entire truth is that it may not be in the way you envisioned. Your heavenly Father will certainly send someone or something to get you back on His track for your life, but at first you may not recognize that particular someone or something as being heaven-sent. You might even believe that your situation has gone from bad to worse, as I'm sure Jonah felt in his case!

If Jonah had imagined he would be given a way of escape, he might have envisioned the sailors throwing him a life preserver as the storm calmed down—but no, that didn't happen. Next, he might have imagined a small fishing boat coming his way with a beautiful girl at the helm—but no, that didn't happen. As the minutes went by, perhaps Jonah dreamed of having super powers so he could miraculously fly from the middle of the ocean to dry ground—but no, that didn't happen. God had a better idea! God sent a great fish to swallow the storm-tossed and very humbled Jonah.

Often, when I am in over my head, I am able to come up with all sorts of great ideas for God to solve the situation. Have you done the same? I create various scenarios that would work well for me, and it is my sad but true history that God has never yet accepted one of my brilliant ideas. Imagine that! God always has a way of escape for this soggy traveler that is very different from what I would have preferred in my wet state.

However, what I do know for Jonah is that there truly are much worse things in life than being swallowed by a massive fish. Never being caught by God would be infinitely worse than spending three nights in the belly of a blimp of a sea creature. Never saying yes to God would be so much more appalling than slogging around in rotting fish guts for seventy-two hours of one's life. Never again hearing the voice of God would be so much more ghastly than smelling the residue of an immense fish's dinner from the night before. Never again being used by God would be so much more nauseating than walking around with the vomit of a marine critter on your tunic.

Give a Little Whistle

[Jonah continued to pray,] *"Water encompassed me to the point of death. The great deep engulfed me, weeds were wrapped around my head. I descended to the roots of the mountains. The earth with its bars was around me forever, but You have brought up my life from the pit, O LORD my God. While I was fainting away, I remembered the LORD, and my prayer came to You, into Your holy temple. Those who regard vain idols forsake their faithfulness, but I will sacrifice to You with the voice of thanksgiving. That which I have vowed I will pay. Salvation is from the LORD."*

—Jonah 2:5–9

Jonah's near-death experience caused him to break out into a hymn of praise even while he was in the middle of the digestive system of the enormous fish. He knew that he had absolutely nothing to complain about and so he took this moment in his life to worship the Lord—even though he didn't know if he would ever leave that place of stomach acids, crushed seafowl, and disgusting odors. Jonah didn't complain and ask God why He hadn't seen fit to rescue him a different way. Instead, this repentant prophet sang loudly, and as the melody echoed through the cavernous rib-cage of the floating beast, Jonah recommitted his life to the Lord.

What is your emotional and spiritual response when the waves of your self-inflicted storm land you in a place you would rather not be? Do you write letters of complaint to the management? Do you shake your fist in the face of the One who has made you and rescued you? Or, do you join Jonah in a chorus of "How Great Thou Art"?

Then the LORD *commanded the fish, and it vomited Jonah up onto the dry land.*   —Jonah 2:10

I love the word *"then"* in this particular verse; it implies that something is about to happen due to an event that has previously occurred. This is what is known as "cause and effect." The Holy Spirit is noting in this verse that there is a relationship between the event of verse 10 and the event described in the preceding verses. What the Spirit recounts through the pen of Jonah in verse 10 is a direct result of Jonah's choice to worship in the darkest and dankest place of his life. Because Jonah worshipped the Lord, the Lord spoke to the fish to get rid of Jonah! Not only did this massive sea monster vomit Jonah up—but he vomited him onto perfectly dry ground. The creature could have expelled him in the middle of the ocean, which is where fish of such enormous size normally stay. But this obedient fish heard the voice of God, swam to the shore, and regurgitated Jonah! What a miraculous series of events!

Now, the next time you wonder if God is able to deliver you from the darkest place you have ever experienced in your life, just start to sing! Give a little whistle! Hum a happy tune! Lift your voice in praise and worship! The God who rescued Jonah by causing him to be swallowed alive by a colossal fish, and then telling that same behemoth to spit Jonah out onto dry ground, is the same God whom you serve today! Never underestimate the power of Jonah's God!

What If?

Now the word of the LORD came to Jonah the second time, saying, "Arise, go to Nineveh the great city and proclaim to it the proclamation which I am going to tell you." So Jonah arose and went to Nineveh according to the word of the LORD. Now Nineveh was an exceedingly great city, a three days' walk. Then Jonah began to go through the city one day's walk; and he cried out and said, "Yet forty days and Nineveh will be overthrown." Then the people of Nineveh believed in God; and they called a fast and put on sackcloth from the greatest to the least of them. —Jonah 3:1–5*

What if God had not pursued Jonah? What if God had left Jonah to die in the storm because he was the one who had caused it in the first place? Why was God so intent upon speaking to Jonah again and using his life at that moment in history?

If God had not pursued Jonah but had left him on the bottom of the ocean floor, then Nineveh, a city of over a hundred thousand people, might have perished. God was intent on speaking to Jonah again and convincing him to obey His instructions simply because He loves people. God pursues us even when we cause violent storms that splash onto the lives of others.

When the Lord convinced Jonah to listen to and obey His voice, it wasn't just about Jonah. It was about God's heart for those who were lost in sin. The same is true for you. When God wants you to hear His voice and obey His instructions, it is not just about you, but it is also about the people in your world who are in desperate need of a Savior.

Your Nineveh

In the year 1748, a fierce storm nearly engulfed a slave ship. The ship's captain was a man by the name of John Newton. During the violent tempest, he was reading *The Imitation of Christ* by Thomas à Kempis. Captain Newton converted to Christianity while his boat was being tossed to and fro by the potent waves of the storm. He eventually became an Anglican clergyman, the author of the beloved hymn "Amazing Grace," and a passionate abolitionist. John Newton's storm wasn't just about John Newton, but it was about the slaves whom God dearly loved and desired to deliver.

Jonah's Nineveh involved a specific location and people group; Captain John Newton's "Nineveh" encompassed the men, women, and children being held in slavery. Each man heard the voice of God during one of the most dreadful experiences of their lives. Although their storms were vicious and nearly fatal, their faith was solidified amid the blasts of the sea, and they completed their divine assignments by ministering to their "Nineveh."

What is your divine assignment, your Nineveh? We all have one, you know. Many of us try to run from it, and yet God pursues us even during the ensuing storms. Each one of us has a group of people to which we have been called; it might be your coworkers or the students in your classroom. It might be certain people in the entertainment industry whom you are called to pray for by name, or the leaders of a foreign country. Your unique calling by the God of Jonah might be the patients on your hospital floor, the families in your neighborhood, or your high school friends. Don't ignore your Nineveh but make a fresh commitment today to embrace your calling and your destiny. Like Jonah, you have been appointed to speak God's Word to this group of people by your walk and by your words.

The Rest of the Story

When the word reached the king of Nineveh, he arose from his throne, laid aside his robe from him, covered himself with sackcloth and sat on the ashes. He issued a proclamation and it said, "In

Nineveh by the decree of the king and his nobles: do not let man, beast, herd, or flock taste a thing. Do not let them eat or drink water. But both man and beast must be covered with sackcloth; and let men call on God earnestly that each may turn from his wicked way and from the violence which is in his hands. Who knows, God may turn and relent and withdraw His burning anger so that we will not perish." When God saw their deeds, that they turned from their wicked way, then God relented concerning the calamity which He had declared He would bring upon them. And He did not do it. —Jonah 3:6–10

The Ninevites repented, and the Lord spared them! And God used a stubborn dude named Jonah to accomplish this. It is reassuring to know that God still uses people who have rejected Him and who have tried to run away from Him. God uses broken, ordinary people for His divine purposes. Keep in mind that the only type of people whom God ever uses are imperfect people who have a list of sins in their past.

You might still wonder if God can use you if you've made mistakes or are dealing with other types of struggles in your life—if you've had an abortion, been divorced, gone through bankruptcy, or have a child who is dealing with addiction. One of the most amazing characteristics about the God whom we serve is that when we make a mistake and run away from Him, He doesn't love us any less than He did before the mistake. When we sin, He doesn't turn away from us but instead comes after us! I believe it is actually our human weaknesses and frailties that qualify us for service in God's kingdom, once we understand that His ways are best and allow Him to take over.

When we are weak—He is strong.

When we fail—He lifts us up.

When we cry—He holds us.

When we sin—He forgives us.

When we say, "I can't"—He declares, "But I can!"

When we run—He pursues us.

When we return to Him—He restores us.

"Spiritual shipwreck rarely happens in a moment.
More often it is the result of slowly drifting from the course
Jesus set before us."

—Garrett Kell

PART FIVE

The Final Answer to All of Your Storm Questions

FOURTEEN

The Difficult "Why?"

As we begin to study the next storm, which is full of heartbreaking events, can I just be honest with you? There is something about the book of Job that troubles me. I am not exactly afraid of it, but neither am I very fond of it. The truth is, I am not sure I want to know *why* Satan targeted Job. I am not sure I want to know *why* bad things happen to good people. The Pollyanna part of me just wants to focus on the powerful fact that God is good all the time and that He is all I need to get through whatever storms I may encounter.

I am not alone in my "hands-off" approach to the book of Job; Christopher Ash, a British theologian, has referred to it as "a neglected treasure of the Christian life." I must hang my head in utter embarrassment and say that I have neglected it because I didn't want to "catch it." Just in case the book of Job is contagious—I want to stay far, far away from it!

But there actually was a man named Job who really did suffer tremendously, even though he was an exceedingly good man. I am not an expert on the book of Job, and I am not sure I would want to be an expert on this very difficult portion of the greatest Book ever written. However, I have diligently studied the forty-two chapters of this Old Testament text, and I believe we can learn stunning lessons from the life of Job—whose troubles all began with Satan and a storm.

Once Upon a Time

> *There was a man in the land of Uz whose name was Job; and that man was* **blameless**, *upright, fearing God and turning away from evil. Seven sons and three daughters were born to him. His possessions also were 7,000 sheep, 3,000 camels, 500 yoke of oxen, 500 female donkeys, and very many servants; and that man was the greatest of all the men of the east.* —Job 1:1–3

From these verses, we can ascertain that Job did everything well; I can guarantee you that he was voted "Most Likely to Succeed" in his graduating class at Uz High School. The Bible uses a strong yet rare adjective to describe this man who is about to meet the storm of the millennium. That adjective is "*blameless.*"

In the *New American Standard Bible*, the word "*blameless*" is used to describe six particular people: Noah, God (including Jesus and the Holy Spirit as members of the triune God), Job, Zacharias, Elizabeth—and you! ("You," of course, refers to all of us as believers who live in the righteousness of Christ!) Certainly, there are others in the Bible who acted blamelessly in singular situations, and there also were those who were challenged to embrace a blameless lifestyle. However, when used as an all-inclusive adjective to describe a person's lifestyle, the word "*blameless*" is reserved for these six whom I have just mentioned: Noah, God, Job, Zacharias, Elizabeth, and you:

> *These are the records of the generations of Noah.* **Noah** *was a righteous man,* **blameless** *in his time; Noah walked with God.* —Genesis 6:9

*As for **God**, His way is **blameless**; the word of the LORD is tested; He is a shield to all who take refuge in Him.*   —2 Samuel 22:31

*In the days of Herod, king of Judea, there was a priest named **Zacharias**, of the division of Abijah; and he had a wife from the daughters of Aaron, and her name was **Elizabeth**. They were both righteous in the sight of God, walking **blamelessly** in all the commandments and requirements of the Lord.*   —Luke 1:5–6

*Blessed be the God and Father of our Lord Jesus Christ, who has blessed us with every spiritual blessing in the heavenly places in Christ, just as He chose us in Him before the foundation of the world, that **we** would be holy and **blameless** before Him.*
        —Ephesians 1:3–4

So, in case you were wondering if you and Job had anything in common, I wanted to begin this storm story by identifying the fact that the Bible describes you both as blameless. Knowing that the Holy Spirit, who is the Author of all truth, went into His bag of words and pulled out the adjective *blameless* in connection with both Job and you leads me to believe that blameless people are not immune to the attack of the enemy. Sin is not the only prerequisite for suffering. Therefore, the next time you observe someone going through a harsh season in life, don't automatically assume they did something to deserve it. Even blameless people encounter the lies of the enemy, as well as his wretched and destructive tactics.

A Family Man

[Job's] sons used to go and hold a feast in the house of each one on his day, and they would send and invite their three sisters to eat and drink with them. When the days of feasting had completed

*their cycle, Job would send and consecrate them, rising up early in
the morning and offering burnt offerings according to the number
of them all; for Job said, "Perhaps my sons have sinned and cursed
God in their hearts." Thus Job did continually.*   —Job 1:4–5

See, I knew that you were going to like Job! He loved his sons, his
daughters, and their families. Just as their sons did, Job and his wife probably hosted family gatherings so they could spend time with their children and grandchildren. Can't you just picture Job sitting at the head of
a massive table, praying over the celebratory meal and then just looking
around at those whom he knew the best and loved the most? I can imagine
the twinkle in his eye as he listened to his sons teasing each other and his
daughters sharing about what one of the grandchildren had accomplished.
Not only was Job blameless, but he was also blessed in every way that a
person could ever hope or aspire to be blessed.

The book of Job was most likely written during the days of the
Patriarchs, which would set this historical account during the days of
Abraham, Isaac, and Jacob. During this particular time in Bible history,
the father was the family's religious leader, and so Job acted as the priest of
his family and was required to offer sacrifices on their behalf and ask for
their forgiveness. Job took this responsibility seriously because he cared
deeply about his children's eternal destiny. Before the coming of Christ
and His death at Calvary, the only way to God was through the blood sacrifice of an animal. Job's highest priority in life was to keep himself and his
family in right relationship with God.

Job was quite the man, who had raised quite the family. But this is not
the end of his story.

"Peace is not the absence of trouble but the presence of Christ."

—Sheila Walsh

FIFTEEN

A Power Struggle

We left Job reclining at the family table and loving every minute of the life that he and God together had built. However, now a storm begins to brew on the horizon of Job's life—and it is going to be a massive one.

Roaming in the Back Alleys

> *Now there was a day when the sons of God came to present them-selves before the LORD, and Satan also come among them. The LORD said to Satan, "From where do you come?" Then Satan answered the LORD and said, "From roaming about on the earth and walking around on it."* —Job 1:6–7

As I picture this scenario, it is almost as if the angels had gathered for a divine cabinet meeting. Somehow, among the spiritual beings in attendance that day was *"Satan."* The word *Satan* is more of a title than a personal name. This evil being is literally Enemy Number One of the people of God. In the Bible, in addition to being called *"Satan"* (see, for example, Luke 11:18), he is variously referred to as our *"adversary"* (1 Peter 5:8), the *"accuser"* (Revelation 12:10), the *"father of lies"* (John 8:44), *"Lucifer"* (Isaiah 14:12 NKJV), the *"devil"* (see, for example, Acts 10:38), the *"prince of the power of the air"* (Ephesians 2:2), the *"ruler of the demons"* (see, for example, Mark 3:22), the *"thief"* (John 10:10), the *"tempter"* (Matthew 4:3; 1 Thessalonians 3:5), the *"evil one"* (Matthew 13:19, 38), a *"roaring lion"* (1 Peter 5:8), and the *"serpent"* (see, for example, Genesis 3:1; Revelation 12:9).

The above verses from the first chapter of Job provide an extremely interesting piece of information concerning the activities of Satan. He had been *"roaming about on the earth."* He had been taking a stroll across the land that God had created, just to see what trouble he could get into. The most exact Hebrew translation of Satan's response to God is, "I have been inspecting Your land."

In the New Testament, Peter gives similar details about how the enemy looks for occasions to spread his malice:

Be of sober spirit, be on the alert. Your adversary, the devil, roams around like a roaring lion, seeking someone to devour.

—1 Peter 5:8

In this verse, written by one of the disciples of Jesus who became a leader in the early church, the Greek verb translated *"roams around"* can mean "to make due use of opportunities." The enemy is an opportunist, and he will take advantage of God's creation in any way imaginable.

Force but No Power

In both the Old Testament and the New Testament, Satan is described as "roaming." However, he had a greater presence and power in the Old Testament. Because of Jesus's life, death at Calvary, and resurrection from the dead, the works of the enemy have been destroyed! This makes it gloriously possible for all of us who are living after the accomplished work of Jesus Christ on the cross to never need to fear the full impact of a Job-like attack on our lives.

For the devil has sinned from the beginning. The Son of God appeared for this purpose, to destroy the works of the devil.

—1 John 3:8

When, on the cross, Jesus shouted, *"It is finished!"* (John 19:30), He was declaring to all of eternity past, to the angels in heaven, and to the demons in hell that He had accomplished what He had been sent to do. He had been sent to destroy the works of the devil—and He had done it! His mission had been victoriously completed!

Satan is still roaming the earth, but he no longer has the same power depicted in the book of Job because Calvary changed everything, for all of eternity. And you, my friend, have been given the authority and power of heaven to defeat him!

*And [Jesus] called the twelve together, and gave them **power** and **authority** over all the demons and to heal diseases.* —Luke 9:1

*Behold I have given you **authority** to tread on serpents and scorpions, and **over all the power of the enemy**, and nothing will injure you.* —Luke 10:19

*But you will receive **power** when the Holy Spirit has come upon you; and you shall be My witnesses both in Jerusalem, and in all Judea and Samaria, and even to the remotest part of the earth.*

—Acts 1:8

*Now may the God of hope fill you with all joy and peace in believing, so that you will abound in hope by the **power** of the Holy Spirit.*   —Romans 15:13

*But we have this treasure in earthen vessels, so that the surpassing greatness of the **power** will be of God and not from ourselves.*
                                                              —2 Corinthians 4:7

*Now to Him who is able to do far more abundantly beyond all that we ask or think, according to the **power** that works within us.*
                                                              —Ephesians 3:20

From these Scriptures, it is clear that God has bequeathed to you, as His child, His glorious power so that you will be able to endure all of the storms that come your way, and even command that the peace of Christ would rule and reign in the midst of a storm.

As a young adult, I was privileged to attend a Christian university where I was not only prepared for a career, but I was also discipled and nurtured in the Word of God and in Christian principles. At that time, I was greatly impacted by the campus pastor, Bob Stamps. "Brother Bob," as the thousands of students affectionately called him, went on to receive his doctorate from Oxford and became a leading voice in evangelical Christianity. I'll never forget a sermon that Brother Bob preached one day in our biweekly chapel service in the mid-1970s. He was teaching Christian leaders of the next generation exactly how to view the enemy:

Because of Calvary and the blood of Jesus Christ, Satan now only has force but no power. He can try to bully you, but he cannot destroy you. He can try to rough you up a bit, but he doesn't have the final say in your life.

I have often thought about these words from Brother Bob in the more than four decades since I first heard them spoken to me as an impressionable young woman of faith: "Satan now only has force but no power."

Calvary ripped the power out of Satan's bag of tricks and left him with only deceit and force. We can discern and steer clear of the enemy's deceit through the truth of God's Word and the guidance of the Holy Spirit. And we can defeat his force in the authority and power of Christ. Oh, he will certainly try to make a power play on your life from time to time, but he is only bluffing—that is all that he is able to do.

Satan may still be hanging around like a juvenile delinquent, loitering in the back alleys of your life. However, my friend, you can overcome his deception because you are the light of the world!

You are the light of the world. A city set on a hill cannot be hidden. —Matthew 5:14

You are the one who has been called, post-Calvary, to shine the light of Christ into the darkened alleyways in which Satan is hanging out! You have the Word of God and the indwelling Spirit to fight against the deceit of the enemy! The storm doesn't have the power—you have the power!

"I've experienced His Presence in the deepest darkest hell
that man can create.... I have tested the promises of the Bible,
and believe me, you can count on them."

—Corrie ten Boom

SIXTEEN

Eavesdropping

It is uniquely fascinating to me that God and Satan actually had a conversation and that the Bible records it word for word. I am not sure why I had never pictured God speaking with Satan before I started studying the book of Job, but I am utterly mesmerized by this exchange of words between Good and Evil. Let's continue to eavesdrop on this verbal exchange between the Creator and the Destroyer:

The LORD said to Satan, "Have you considered My servant Job? For there is no one like him on the earth, a blameless and upright man, fearing God and turning away from evil." —Job 1:8

God knew the character of Job. He was intimately acquainted with His servant and all of his ways—just as he is with me and my ways, and with you and your ways. God knew that no matter what Satan did to Job, this one-of-a-kind man would still be found blameless.

Satan, however, was in direct disagreement with God's opinion of Job:

Then Satan answered the Lord, *"Does Job fear God for nothing?*
Have You not made a hedge about him and his house and all that
he has, on every side? You have blessed the work of his hands, and
his possessions have increased in the land. But put forth Your hand
now and touch all that he has; he will surely curse You to Your
face." —Job 1:9–11

It is clear that Satan was unimpressed with God's assessment of His servant. The devil's discernment (which is never reliable) was that Job was a fair-weather friend of God. We can almost hear the sarcastic sneer in Satan's voice as he disagrees with God on the subject of Job's faithfulness. Satan believed that Job followed the Lord solely because he had received material blessings and riches from Him. In Satan's "expert" estimation, Job trusted God only because God had insulated him.

Then the Lord *said to Satan, "Behold, all that he has is in your*
power, only do not put forth your hand on him." So Satan departed
from the presence of the Lord. —Job 1:12

It is shocking that God gave Satan permission to stretch out his hand against Job! It's true that God warned the enemy not to directly touch Job's life, but everything else around him was fair game.

The suffering that Job is about to endure is not given as a punishment for any sin in his life or any mistake that he has made. It seems that the suffering the enemy was allowed to throw at Job was a divinely approved test. The God of the universe wanted to prove to Mr. Deceit that Job would worship Him despite undergoing intense suffering. God didn't have to give permission to the enemy to do this, but He did. In His infinite goodness and inscrutable wisdom, the Lord was willing to allow the enemy to test His servant. Moreover, God was always in total control of the situation; Satan's power was, and always has been, subservient to God's.

Job's storm changed the trajectory of his entire life. It also changed the perspective of God's people on suffering from that time forward. This test has taught us all how to suffer well and how to expect the compassion of God to write the last chapter in all of our stories.

Staccato Attack

Now on the day when his sons and his daughters were eating and drinking wine in their oldest brother's house, a messenger came to Job and said, "The oxen were plowing and the donkeys feeding beside them, and the Sabeans attacked and took them. They also slew the servants with the edge of the sword, and I alone have escaped to tell you." While he was still speaking, another also came and said, "The fire of God fell from heaven and burned up the sheep and the servants and consumed them, and I alone have escaped to tell you." While he was still speaking, another also came and said, "The Chaldeans formed three bands and made a raid on the camels and took them and slew the servants with the edge of the sword, and I alone have escaped to tell you." While he was still speaking, another also came and said, "Your sons and your daughters were eating and drinking wine in their oldest brother's house, and behold, a great wind came from across the wilderness and struck the four corners of the house, and it fell on the young people and they died, and I alone have escaped to tell you."

—Job 1:13–19

Do you feel the staccato of attack in this passage? Whenever I read it, my eyes bounce back and forth as if I am watching a Wimbledon tennis match. I can't take it all in as scenario after devastating scenario is communicated to Job in a matter of minutes. It is too much for one man to take! My heart is in my throat as I wrestle with Job's horror and the stark devastation that has occurred in his life. But I am even more anxious to discover whose assessment of Job will turn out to be correct—God's or Satan's.

What Is a Person to Do?

Then Job arose and tore his robe and shaved his head, and he fell to the ground and worshiped. —Job 1:20

God was right! (As He always is, I might add.) The enemy was sorely mistaken in his opinion about Job's motivations for serving the Lord. How wrong he was then, and how wrong he is now about God's faithful servants! In spite of catastrophe, devastation, and unmatched human affliction, Job fell to the ground and worshipped the Lord! I am weeping as I write these words and as the life-altering lessons of Job's storms are absorbed into my impressionable heart. Our first response after experiencing a category 5 hurricane in life should always be to fall to our knees and break out in worship.

As we study the ensuing life of Job, we will see that he experienced days of questioning and wondering. We will see that Job wept and grieved; he suffered from a broken heart ravaged by his spasms of mourning. We understand that kind of response. What is often hard for us to understand is his first response of worship.

We somehow take consolation in the fact that many people mourn and whine and grieve loudly when they are in the midst of a storm because we want to be given the same opportunity when our time comes. However, when we meet a man or a woman who has processed their anguish through worship, that often offends us. We wonder if they are "stuffing" their pain or even ignoring it. But from the life of Job, we can observe that it is possible to worship your way through suffering.

[Job] *said, "Naked I came from my mother's womb, and naked I shall return there. The* LORD *gave and the* LORD *has taken away. Blessed be the name of the* LORD.*" Through all this Job did not sin nor did he blame God.* —Job 1:21–22

Oh, that this passage of Scripture would be the testimony of my life! Oh, that this passage of Scripture would be the testimony of all of our lives! Oh, that each one of us would bow down before God and worship at the very worst moments of our lives!

Job did not sin as he surveyed the condition of his life from the position of his knees. He didn't blame God but instead blessed Him. The final verse of the first chapter of Job implies that blaming God is considered a sin from heaven's point of view. It is possible to grieve fully and completely without blaming God for your pain. Grief is an acceptable human emotion; there is no sin inherent in enduring a broken heart. Sin is birthed when the creation blames the Creator.

To Blame or to Bless—That Is the Question

Job is not the only one in the Bible who chose to worship the Lord even when in the depths of despair. When David lost his infant son to a fatal illness, he chose to worship the Lord as well:

But when David saw that his servants were whispering together, David perceived that the child was dead; so David said to his servants, "Is the child dead?" And they said, "He is dead." So David arose from the ground, washed, anointed himself, and changed his clothes; and he came into the house of the LORD and worshiped. Then he came to his own house, and when he requested, they set food before him and he ate. —2 Samuel 12:19–20

David worshipped after the death of his baby boy, and Job worshipped as he grieved the loss of all his children. Each of us is faced with profound choices when dealing with the aftermath of a life storm, but the most important decision is this: *Will you blame God or will you bless God?*

The storm that you have been walking through is actually a test of blame or blessing. When the enemy sends a violent tempest into your life, you are handed a test paper. The test consists of one simple question that includes two options to choose from:

What will you do when your life has been razed by a horrid and monstrous storm? (Choose one)

___ Bless the Lord

___ Blame the Lord

The enemy will endeavor to convince you to blame the Lord, but blameless people bless the Lord! There is no blame in a blameless person, so when cruel conditions caused by a cyclone invade your life, purpose to live in the righteousness of Christ, fall to your knees, and bless the Lord! The best way to observe storm damage is from the position of your knees.

The storms in life will always reveal if there is any blame in your heart or in your relationship to the Lord. How you respond to the demolition that a squall causes reveals the condition of your heart; it is a litmus test of your intimacy with God.

Worship transcends comprehension; you don't need to "understand" what is happening in your life in order to worship the Lord. We all deal with situations that cause grief to well up within our souls; none of us is a stranger to those life events in which sorrow threatens to overwhelm us. However, let's learn from the examples of David and Job. If all you do during the grief process is to weep, then you are doing only half the job. You can weep—but please worship too! You can cry from human pain—but cry out to the Lord as well! I can assure you that God will take every cry of human grief that you have uttered and combine them with every song of praise that you have sacrificed, and He will create a glorious and eternal symphony.

When you worship the Lord in the aftermath of the storm and gain the perspective that staying on your knees brings, you will find that the healing has begun.

"Extraordinary afflictions are not always the punishment of extraordinary sins but sometimes the trail of extraordinary graces. God hath many sharp-cutting instruments and rough files for the polishing of His jewels; and those He especially loves, and means to make the most resplendent, He hath oftenest His tools upon."

—Archbishop Leighton

SEVENTEEN

It's Not Over 'Til It's Over

The enemy is a weak, whining entity and has so few capabilities that it is nearly laughable. However, we know that he does possess the ability to deceive. He also has the uncanny trait of never giving up. His relentless nature has caused a heap of trouble and agony for God's people since the beginning of time. This spiritual persona of evil has the tenacity and audacity to go after God's people again and again. So it was with Job, and so it will be with you and me. Often, when we make it through a ferocious storm, we fall into the false belief that we are now safe for a while; however, that is not what the deceiver is thinking at all.

At It Again

Again there was a day when the sons of God came to present themselves before the LORD, and Satan also came among them to present himself before the LORD. The LORD said to Satan, "Where have you come from?" Then Satan answered the LORD and said,

"From roaming about on the earth and walking around on it." The
LORD said to Satan, "Have you considered My servant Job? For
there is no one like him on the earth, a blameless and upright man
fearing God and turning away from evil. And he still holds fast his
integrity, although you incited Me against him to ruin him without
cause."

—Job 2:1–3

Satan is at it again! The enemy is not easily discouraged, but often
chooses to torment us when we are at our very lowest. He is waging war
against Job, and the second fierce battle is about to begin.

Satan answered the LORD and said, "Skin for skin! Yes, all that
a man has he will give for his life. However, put forth Your hand
now, and touch his bone and his flesh; he will curse You to Your
face." So the LORD said to Satan, "Behold, he is in your power,
only spare his life."

—Job 2:4–6

Satan was unimpressed with Job's integrity and heart for the Lord;
however he did decide to change his strategy. The enemy's first technique
(governed by God's restriction) had been to attack Job's family and all that
he owned. But Job worshipped his way through the grief and sorrow of that
unexpected and undeserved first blast. Therefore, this time, Satan asked
permission to go for the jugular—Job's own flesh. The enemy believed that
if he could cause Job physical pain, rather than only emotional trauma,
then Job would turn his back on God and even curse his Creator.

The Storm Intensifies

Then Satan went out from the presence of the LORD and smote Job
with sore boils from the sole of his foot to the crown of his head.

—Job 2:7

The enemy struck Job with unimaginable and abhorrent human suffering. Job woke up one morning with boils all over his body—there was not one inch of skin that was free of these ugly, crusty, and painful abscesses. As if torturing Job emotionally and mentally had not been enough, Satan had now afflicted this godly man with such excruciating physical pain that there was not one moment of the night or day when he felt the least bit of relief.

And [Job] took a potsherd to scrape himself while he was sitting among the ashes. Then his wife said to him, "Do you still hold fast your integrity? Curse God and die!" But he said to her, "You speak as one of the foolish women speaks. Shall we indeed accept good from God and not accept adversity?" In all this Job did not sin with his lips.　　　　　　　　　　　　　　　—Job 2:8–10

As evidenced by the conversation Job had with his wife at the onset of his wretched and burning physical condition, his faith is still holding up. Satan's chief goal in attacking Job with this epic storm was to convince Job to doubt God. Yet the Bible clearly states that in response to this second wave of torment, *"Job did not sin with his lips."*

That is the challenge we all face during a violent storm, isn't it? It is the challenge not to sin with our lips. The greatest test we will be forced to pass while enduring a torrential downpour with windy blasts is to guard very closely what comes out of our mouths. There will be people, like Job's wife, who essentially try to convince us to curse God. However, know that the result of cursing God is always death. If you begin to blame God for the storm that is attempting to devour your very existence, you might not die a physical death, but you will certainly start to die a spiritual and emotional death. What comes out of your mouth at the worst moment of your life is perhaps the most telling about the authenticity of your faith.

Will you break out in song when the winds and hail are battering your safety? Will you worship God when atmospheric conditions are causing you immense misery? Or will you curse God and die? The level of our faith is always determined not only by what we believe and think, but also by what we say—especially during times of onslaught by the circumstances of life.

The Fellowship of His Suffering

As a woman of God and a woman called to ministry, I have been greatly impacted by the teachings and writings of Elisabeth Elliot. Elisabeth was a young wife and mother when the Auca Indians slaughtered her missionary husband, Jim. Elisabeth wrote a powerful book entitled *Through Gates of Splendor* that chronicles this twentieth-century event. Countless men and women have been called to serve God on the foreign mission field due to the testimony of Jim and Elisabeth Elliot.

When I was in college, Elisabeth had recently written a book called *Let Me Be a Woman: Notes to My Daughter on the Meaning of Womanhood*. This book became my blueprint for both femininity and morality. (More than forty years later, I still have my very first copy of this book, and I have also given copies of it to many young women across the decades of my life.)

Later, when I was a young mother of five rambunctious children whom I was attempting to homeschool, I would often send all of them outside to play for half an hour at ten o'clock on a weekday morning while other children were learning long division or Latin conjugation. During the thirty minutes that followed, my creative learners would be pretending to be pioneers in the backyard or having an intense championship basketball game in the driveway of our home. While my loud, lively brood was engaged in play, I would be sitting in our van in the driveway listening to Elisabeth Elliot on the radio. For some reason, I was not able to listen to the Christian station that sponsored her program from the radio inside the house, but it came in loud and clear in the McLeod-mobile.

From Elisabeth, I learned how to be a servant in the home and how to rejoice even when my life was hard. She taught me how to find joy in the daily activities of mothering and encouraged my weary soul when I didn't know if I could carry on for one more day. She read the poetry of the saints who had gone before us and told stories of those who had served the Lord in spite of arduous disappointment. I learned how to be a woman of God from Elisabeth Elliot.

Elisabeth would answer every question with these words: "What does the Bible say?" That question has become my motto and mantra in all of the years that have flown by.

As my life has become less demanding on the home front, I have continued to be transformed and strengthened by the writings of Elisabeth Elliot Leitch Gren—who lost not just one husband to death, but two. Her views on suffering have offered a solid anchor to this storm-tossed sailor through all of life's gusting winds and pounding waves.

In her well-loved book *Keep a Quiet Heart*, which is a compilation of articles from her newsletter, Elisabeth addresses the topic of Christian suffering. This stalwart and faithful woman knows the call of suffering. The following words are taken from the chapter entitled "Love's Sacrifice Leads to Joy":

> Easter, the most joyful of all Christian feast days, follows that most sorrowful of days we remember. The joy of Easter proceeds from the Cross. Without Christ's pouring out of His soul to death there would have been no resurrection. We cannot know Christ and the power of His resurrection without also entering into the fellowship of His suffering.
>
> For years I have had on the wall of my study these lines written by one Ugo Bassi: "Measure thy life by loss instead of gain.... Love's strength standeth in Love's sacrifice." Those lines epitomize the central teaching of the Lord Jesus—that life springs forth from death.... They speak to the timeworn question, *Why, Lord?* [4]

---

4. Quotations from Elisabeth Elliot in this chapter are taken from *Keep a Quiet Heart* (Fleming Revell, 2006), 64–68. Italics are in the original.

Elisabeth then summarizes a sermon that was preached by Ugo Bassi, who was a priest during the nineteenth century. One of his places of assignment was a hospital rife with suffering. It was there that he preached to those who needed comfort from their physical pain.

Bassi chose the Vineyard chapter, John 15, as his text, showing that the life of the Vine is "not of pleasure nor of ease." Almost before the flower fades the fruit begins to grow, but instead of being allowed to grow where it will, it is tied immediately to a stake, forced to draw out of the hard hillside its nourishment. When "the fair shoots begin to wind and wave in the blue air, and feel how sweet it is," along comes the gardener with pruning hooks and shears, "and strips it bare of all its innocent pride...and cuts deep and sure, unsparing for its tenderness and joy."

How I can relate to the life of the vine! There have been times when I have felt that the fruit I was producing was beneficial to others and even delicious, but as My Gardener has examined my life, He has made a very painful decision on my behalf. He has pruned my life so drastically that I, too, have been stripped bare and been tempted to believe that all joy is gone.

Bassi goes on to describe the vintage, when the vine bends low with the weight of the grapes, "wrought out of the long striving of its heart." But ah! the hands are ready to tear down the treasures of the grapes; the feet are there to tread them in the wine-press "until the blood-red rivers of the wine run over, and the land is full of joy. But the vine standeth stripped and desolate, having given all, and now its own dark time is come, and no man payeth back to it the comfort and the glory of its gift." Winter comes, and the vine is cut back to the very stem (I had not known, as John and Jesus and Bassi knew, how terribly drastic is the pruning process), "despoiled, disfigured, left a leafless stock, alone through all the dark days that shall come."

While the vine undergoes this death, the wine it has produced is gladdening the heart of man. Have you, perhaps, like the vine, given happiness to others, yet found yourself seemingly forsaken? Has it made you bitter? We need the paradigm of the vine, which is "not bitter for the torment undergone, not barren for the fullness yielded up.... The Vine from every living limb bleeds wine; is it the poorer for that spirit shed?"

It is from this context and this joyful truth that the lines Elisabeth had hanging on the wall of her study came:

Measure thy life by loss instead of gain;

Not by the wine drunk but by the wine poured forth;

For love's strength standeth in love's sacrifice,

And whoso suffers most hath most to give.

Perhaps you and I and Elisabeth and Job have been chosen to suffer much because we have much to give. I often remind myself that the Son of God was made perfect through suffering and that He was truly the *"man of sorrows and acquainted with grief"* (Isaiah 53:3). Because I sometimes get spiritual amnesia, I whisper, times without number, to my weakened soul,

But to the degree that you share the sufferings of Christ, keep on rejoicing, so that also at the revelation of His glory you may rejoice with exultation. —1 Peter 4:13

There is a call that is birthed from deep in the eye of the storm, and it is a call that echoes across the intensity and unfamiliarity of the billows.

Once more, it is the call to *worship*—it is to rejoice in spite of a pain so enormous that it threatens to disrupt your very life.

Elisabeth ends this essay by saying,

> The poem [by Bassi] ends with lines for those who cannot feel His presence or see His face. This darkness is the one last trial.
>
> > Christ was forsaken, so must thou be too.
> > Thou wilt not see the face nor feel the hand.
> > Only the cruel crushing of the feet,
> > When through the bitter night the Lord comes down
> > To tread the winepress.—Not by sight, but faith,
> > Endure, endure,—be faithful to the end!
>
> Jesus' word "remain" or "abide" (in Him, in His love), repeated ten times in John 15, means being at home in Him, living constantly in His presence and in harmony with His will. It does not at all mean unmitigated suffering (the vine isn't cut back every day!). For those of us who are not at the moment in pain, may we not let slip any cross Jesus may present to us, any little way of letting go of ourselves, any smallest task to do with gladness and humility, any disappointment accepted with grace and silence. These are His appointments. If we miss them here, we'll not find them again in this world or in any other.

Even when suffering the mighty gales of a storm-tossed life, I choose to live constantly in God's presence. I choose to make myself at home with Him and not with my feelings. I choose to let go of myself and of my preferences so that I can embrace His appointments as joy!

"I bear my willing witness that I owe more to the fire, and the hammer, and the file, than to anything else in my Lord's workshop. I sometimes question whether I have ever learned anything except through the rod. When my schoolroom is darkened, I see most."

—Charles H. Spurgeon

EIGHTEEN

Choosing Friends Wisely

We all have a story, don't we? My story has included depression, infertility, and cancer. Although I would never choose to walk through any of those particular storms again, I can tell you that I am a stronger and more vibrant woman simply because I survived. However, not only did I survive, but I have thrived because of my defiant choice to worship in the storm. Although the call of the storm is to ignore His voice and to refuse His shelter, I have stayed in His presence where there is always fullness of joy. It's not been an easy choice or a simple decision, but it has been the most valuable and the most sustaining decision of my entire life. I dare you to embrace it as well!

Knowing God's Will

When I was in my late twenties and early thirties, I suffered the loss of five babies at between twelve and twenty weeks in my pregnancies. As I described earlier in chapter 6, I held four of those precious little ones in the palm of my hand. The emotional pain was devastating and the depression that engulfed my soul was perpetual and pernicious. Many days, during those seven years of loss and tears, it felt like I could barely breathe. My only reason for getting out of bed in the morning was to take care of my two lively boys, who needed their mama's love and attention.

After losing my fourth baby at nearly twenty weeks into my pregnancy, I stayed at home until, after a week or two, I finally ventured back to church. My husband was the pastor of a small church, and I was hoping for encouragement and compassion from those who had been standing with me in faith for this little one's life. By the end of the service, although I was comforted by the worship and given hope by the sermon, I was still raw with disappointment and grief.

The wife of one of the elders at our church headed straight toward me after the closing "Amen" and wrapped me in her arms. My makeup had all been washed away by my tears, and I was still wearing maternity garments because they were the only clothes that fit me. She looked gorgeous from the top of her well-coiffed hair, to her designer clothes, to her perfectly pedicured toes.

At the end of our sweet hug, she looked me in the face and declared, "Well, now you know it is not God's will."

Innocently, I said to her, "What is not God's will?"

"For you to have another baby," was her callous and quick reply.

I had no words to respond to her, so I just quietly walked away—but I wanted to punch her in the nose! I had a hard time not turning around and blaring my thoughts into her gorgeous face: *No! I don't know that, and neither do you!*

Three Unforgettable Friends

Choosing which friends to gather around you and speak into your life when facing a fierce storm is perhaps one of the most important decisions you will ever make. Nothing impacts your life to a greater degree than who is in your life during and after a cyclone of trauma and chaos.

Job had friends—he had faithful friends—but even they were at a loss as to what to say and do for this man whose life had been so tremendously battered by painful blasts:

Now when Job's three friends heard of all this adversity that had come upon him, they came each one from his own place, Eliphaz the Temanite, Bildad the Shuhite and Zophar the Naamathite; and they made an appointment together to come to sympathize with him and comfort him. When they lifted up their eyes at a distance and did not recognize him, they raised their voices and wept. And each of them tore his robe and they threw dust over their heads toward the sky. Then they sat down on the ground with him for seven days and seven nights with no one speaking a word to him, for they saw that his pain was very great. —Job 2:11–13

The Bible states that in the aftermath of Job's terrifying life storm, his friends came *"to sympathize with him and comfort him."* In visiting Job, these loyal friends apparently had no other agenda than to show sympathy and to be comforters. When people's lives have been decimated due to the high winds of circumstances and the tidal waves of tragedy, they don't need human philosophy, pat answers, or personal opinions. They need what Job's friends initially came to offer. As we help others face appalling devastation, we should be reminded of these two powerful words: *sympathy* and *comfort*.

One of the most striking details about the initial response of Job's friends is that they didn't speak—they didn't say one word to him. These men were so taken by the intensity of their friend's pain that they didn't philosophize, nor did they throw out easy answers. They didn't even verbally offer their condolences. They just *sat* with him.

This response should deliver a lasting reminder to anyone who has a friend dealing with the effects of a difficult season in life: perhaps what is *not* said is much more significant than what *is* said. "Showing up" is more comforting than "showing off." You don't need to have all of the philosophical or theological answers when you go to be with a friend whose life has recently imploded. You just need to sit, and perhaps listen. You just need to pass the tissues and hold their hand.

How I wish that this was the end of the story of Job's friends—but it's not. These three men should have kept their lips locked, but what happened next is nearly as painful as the initial storm.

The Three Stooges

As Job begins to grieve out loud in the safety of the presence of these three men, their reaction is reprehensible. Eliphaz insists that Job must have done something to deserve this treatment and that he should repent:

> *Remember now, who ever perished being innocent? Or where were the upright destroyed? According to what I have seen, those who plow iniquity and those who sow trouble harvest it. By the breath of God they perish, and by the blast of His anger they come to an end.* —Job 4:7–9

Job is incredulous that his dear friend Eliphaz would have the audacity to accuse him of such sin, and so he responds with these words:

> *For the despairing man there should be kindness from his friend; so that he does not forsake the fear [reverence] of the Almighty.* —Job 6:14

If you remember nothing else from the story of Job, remember these words. If God has called you to walk beside someone who is in abject and indescribable agony, just be kind. Kindness is a comforting blanket that comes from those who exhibit godly intentionality toward others who have been tormented and injured. Remember that your friends don't need you to offer theology or seemingly wise answers. They just need your presence, your kindness, and your friendship.

However, Bildad, not to be outdone, had to chime in concerning his own "insight" into the life of Job. His opinion was that God rewards the good; therefore, Job must not be good! Bildad's false assumption was that if Job were a good man, he wouldn't be going through this storm:

Does God pervert justice? Or does the Almighty pervert what is right? If your sons sinned against Him, then He delivered them into the power of their transgression. If you would seek God and implore the compassion of the Almighty, if you are pure and upright, surely now He would rouse Himself for you and restore your righteous estate. —Job 8:3–6

With friends like these, who needs enemies! Bildad actually stated that Job's sons had died because of their sins. Job had already told his friends, between great gulps of weeping and grieving, that what he needed was their kindness, not their opinions. Yet Bildad continued his accusatory discourse with this false assumption about Job:

So are the paths of all who forget God; and the hope of the godless will perish, whose confidence is fragile, and whose trust is a spider's web. He trusts in his house, but it does not stand; he holds fast to it, but it does not endure. —Job 8:13–15

Bildad erroneously accused Job of not trusting in God for his future. With that supposition, he implied that if Job had trusted God to a greater degree, then this calamity would not have come upon him.

In chapter after chapter of the book of Job, I have read the unfeeling words spoken by these three men, and I have imagined the unmitigated pain they caused their friend. When reading Job's response to them, I can't help but blame Eliphaz, Bildad, and Zophar when Job begins to question why God has allowed him to experience such unmatched human tragedy. Before these three "stooges" began to speak, Job did not blame God but instead chose to worship Him. Yet as his friends gave their jaded opinions, he began to wallow in self-pity. And honestly, who can blame him? However, one must wonder what Job's emotional and spiritual response would have been if he'd had friends who encouraged him in his faith and gave him hope at the darkest moment of his life.

It is true that no one is perfect, and our friends will not respond perfectly to the tornadoes that strike our lives. Do you remember my story from the beginning of this chapter about the elder's wife who informed me what she thought was God's will for my life during a time of great personal pain? Do you know what I learned from that situation? I learned to forgive people ahead of time for every "wrong" thing they are going to say. I learned to go to God, rather than to other people, with my deepest questions. I determined that I would not allow the inconsiderate words or actions of others to do any lifelong damage to me. I also decided that when others were blaming God, I would continue to lift up the name of Jesus with my highest praise!

Let's Make It Personal

How can we apply the lessons we learn from observing the reactions of Job's friends? We all have our own friends who are dealing with human pain, and we must be a voice of hope, comfort, and faith to them when debilitating circumstances have razed their lives. There is no place for blame or accusation if you truly long to help a friend rebuild their broken life. If you have ever had to watch someone you dearly love go through uncertainty, devastating pain, and years of sorrow, then the heartbreak for you, as their friend, can also be astronomical. For me, my gut instinct is to strongly desire to save them from their personal storm. But there are many times when we just feel helpless to do anything for a suffering friend.

Yet in the midst of our friend's pain—and its effects on other people around them—somebody has to do something. Someone has to come forward and be a voice of practical blessing. As a pastor's wife for forty years and as a woman who has watched other mothers lose their children through death, who has observed the devastation that follows adultery and divorce, and who has been privy to the desolation inflicted by various types of cancer, I have a practical list of three points that I often refer to when

I am the one called to help a friend pick up the pieces after a particularly difficult storm.

1. *Remind yourself of what an honor it is to be called alongside your friend as they undergo a wretched storm in life.* God looked around and chose you to be a voice of hope. God looked around and chose you to be a calming influence. God looked around and chose you to be a prayer warrior. This is among the highest honors He can bestow upon a person—the calling to help someone who is racked with deep disappointment and life-altering sorrow. Don't ignore this call or walk away from it.

Greater love has no one than this, that one lay down his life for his friends. —John 15:13

2. *Don't just say that you will pray—but actually pray.* When someone else is in the heat of battle, your prayers have the miraculous power to extinguish their flames. Your heartfelt, perpetual prayers have the capacity to lessen the intensity of the heat they are facing. Prayer has the divine ability to strengthen, comfort, heal, soothe, restore joy, and deliver!

Pray for one another so that you may be healed. The effective prayer of a righteous man can accomplish much. —James 5:16

3. *Show up and simply be a friend.* You might need to put other things aside during a storm season in a friend's life so that you can exhibit heartfelt and supportive friendship. You might need to choose friendship with this fragile friend over entertainment, business, or other preferences. Take a meal to their home or send an encouraging e-mail. Perhaps you could hire a cleaning service for their home or, if you can't afford it by yourself, gather a group of friends to help with the cost. Send them flowers or buy them a gift card to a favorite restaurant. Consider babysitting for their children or buying them groceries. You could water their plants or fill up their car with gasoline. Be the hands and feet of Jesus when a friend is in a spiritual intensive care unit! Be Jesus with skin on!

It is during moments in life like this that a true friend doesn't just speak of friendship but demonstrates the consummate show-and-tell of friendship.

Truly I say to you, to the extent that you did it to one of these brothers of Mine, even the least of them, you did it to Me.

—Matthew 25:40

4. *Be a voice of hope in the hopeless situation.* Don't tell your friend horror stories about their situation, like Job's friends did, but be a voice of hope! Don't worry out loud with your discouraged friend, but be a voice of hope! Don't agree with your friend about how bad it looks—be a voice of hope! Send them text messages filled with hopeful Bible verses or mail them a card each day for an entire month with an encouraging Scripture verse on it. You might consider e-mailing them the lyrics of powerful hymns of faith. Help this discouraged and weary soldier to dream again and to think about the good future God has for them.

A joyful heart is good medicine.   —Proverbs 17:22

"The next best thing to being wise oneself is to live in a circle of those who are."

—C. S. Lewis

NINETEEN

The Response of a Storm-Tossed Man

When a friend critiques you, filets you, and accuses you while *you* are the one going through a violent storm, what should your response be? Should you withdraw in emotional pain? Should you throw daggers back at the accuser? Should you humiliatingly agree with their cruel assumptions?

When I was diagnosed with cancer, I had so many precious friends who were supportive and spoke words of encouragement over my life. However, just like Job, I had some "comforters" who knocked on my door only to accuse, criticize, or pontificate. One day, during the pelting downpour of cancer, I received an e-mail from a college acquaintance whom I had not heard from in years. In her e-mail, she stated that she had heard I'd been diagnosed with breast cancer and offered her thoughts and prayers. But then, she injected these very hurtful words: "It has been my experience in ministry that breast cancer is a result of unforgiveness in one's heart. Is there anyone that you need to forgive? If you can forgive, you will certainly be healed."

As you can imagine, those were not the words I needed to hear at that moment.

Words

As we continue to observe Job's life, his true heart will be revealed by the very words he speaks. God has allowed Satan to strip Job completely bare of his ten children, his wealth, and his health. The enemy—the one who roams around on planet earth seeking to devour people—has divested Job of everything he deemed precious, of whatever had any significance to him, and of all that he had achieved. Yet when Job's life is peeled back to its core, we will observe a man of infinite value and pure gold. We will see two incredible marks of a person who truly loves God: he will continue to worship in spite of torturous human pain, and he will continue to trust his Creator even in the face of ruin and trauma. Although Job's outer self is covered with ugly, crusty boils, his inner self reflects a person who is deeply right with God.

Let's listen in now to Job's response to his foolish triumvirate of friends. Although we will not study every word Job speaks, we will examine the theme of his words and the message of his heart. Job utters some difficult phrases and arguments that we are unable to cover in this study; however, the ones I have chosen to point out are certainly indicative of his search for God in the middle of his agony.

A Better Idea

With [God] are wisdom and might; to Him belong counsel and understanding.... Behold, He restrains the waters, and they dry up; and He sends them out, and they inundate the earth.

—Job 12:13, 15

In spite of the heinous pain that has attacked his life, Job simply indicates that all wisdom is from God and not from those whom He has created. He looked his foolish friends in the face and said, in effect, "Guys, I don't have a better idea than God does! Although I don't understand what He is doing, I trust His eternal understanding. He has the power and the wisdom to order the days of my life."

Job wanted these men with small minds and even tinier hearts to realize that because we are human, we have definite limits in our ability to understand the heart and ways of God. However, what we can begin to comprehend, even in our curbed perception, is that God is good no matter what happens and that He is infinitely wise.

With Him are strength and sound wisdom, the misled and the misleader belong to Him. —Job 12:16

As I try to extract Job's message from the above words, I can actually begin to smile! Our friend Job has a sense of humor even in the midst of this once-in-a-lifetime storm. In attempting to jerk his three amigos away from heretical thinking, he identifies himself as the *"misled"* and them as the *"misleader[s]."* He reminds these simpletons that we belong to God even when we have it all wrong! Job knows deep within his soul that God has the power to intervene in our life circumstances and that He has all of the wisdom we could ever possibly require.

No Matter What!

In each of our lives, there comes a defining moment when we must decide that no matter what happens, no matter how others treat us, no matter how desperately difficult our circumstances may become—we will trust God. Generally, it is during a storm in one's life that this decision is tested and refined. Job had made this resolution years earlier, but it was during the most violent portion of his life that he audibly and emphatically declared his internal belief system:

Though He slay me, I will hope in Him. —Job 13:15

These nine words, spoken by a man who lived thousands of years ago, have become the guiding motto and declaration of believers in every generation who experience human havoc. The "spirit of Job" rose up within the man called Job and affirmed, "No matter what happens in my life, I will trust God!"

Have you made that determination in your life? Or have you given in emotionally to the violence and turmoil of the storm? Are you listening to the foolishness of others rather than to the voice of God in your life? The belief system of every man and woman who has chosen to trust in Jesus Christ is tested during days of ravaging storms and life-threatening gales. You and I, along with Job, must make this "No Matter What" resolution, so that we can say:

"No matter how difficult my circumstances are—I will trust God!"

"No matter how long I walk through the valley of the shadow of death—I will trust God!"

"No matter what my finances are—I will trust God!"

"No matter what my health is—I will trust God!"

"No matter what my friends say—I will trust God!"

"No matter how I am treated by others—I will trust God!"

"No matter what choices my children make—I will trust God!"

"No matter how strong this wind is and how long it lasts—I will trust God!"

"No matter how this turns out—I will trust God!"

Life's storms have the hidden ability to reveal the strength of our character and the true belief system of our hearts. Job's character was found to be of pure gold; his faith stood radiant and strong in the calamitous storm. (See 1 Peter 1:7.)

The "Why?" of the Storm

In the middle of a storm, it is not a sin to go to God—your Creator, Comforter, Savior, and Friend—with your deepest questions and darkest pain. Job the blameless knew that in order to survive this wretched time in his life, he must be able to appeal to God in his agony and ask Him two simple questions: "Why?" and "Where are You?"

Those are the questions that any storm in life has the power to stir up in our emotions and in our theology. Physical storms in nature often stir up leaves and branches. A particularly violent gust might even uproot trees and remove roofs from homes. Similarly, spiritual storms have the sudden power to uproot deep questions from within ordinary men and women that they have never asked before.

Immediately after Job declared that no matter what happened in life, he would continue to trust the Lord—"*Though He slay me, I will hope in Him*"— he spoke these desperate words:

Nevertheless I will argue my ways before Him. This also will be my salvation, for a godless man may not come before His presence.   —Job 13:15–16

Job was telling his friends that the very fact that he would ask God questions proved that he did, indeed, believe in God. And he was saying to the Lord, in effect, "Either You are God or You are not!"

This man was crying out from the depths of his belief system. He petitioned the One who made him, "I believe in You, and that is why this hurts so much! I trust You to take care of me, and that is why I don't understand what I am going through!"

No one can argue with Job's interview of God. Often, we have wanted to be brave enough to challenge God with the very same questions. Job had the holy audacity to bring his theological conundrum to the Lord because he did, indeed, believe! He believed in God, and that is the very reason why he went into His holy presence with the questions that were aroused by the storm.

The Creator is not afraid of our questions, and He is not intimidated by our indignation. God *wants* us "in His face"! It is the safest and most sacred place to be while dealing with the aftermath of a wicked tempest in life. Job brought his case to God—and so should you. He appealed to his Creator—and so should you. Job knew that he was only a little man, but God was the only One wise enough and understanding enough to give him the answers he desired and deserved. Where else would we go but to our Creator?

Previously, Job had listed all that God is capable of doing. He can remove mountains and cause the earth to shake and tremble. He can command the sun not to shine and trample down the waves of the seas. Then, Job asserts:

Who does great things, unfathomable, and wondrous works without number. Were He to pass by me, I would not see Him; were He to move past me, I would not perceive Him. Were he to snatch away, who could restrain Him? Who could say to Him, "What are You doing?"... How then can I answer Him, and choose my words before Him? For though I were right, I could not answer; I would have to implore the mercy of my judge. —Job 9:10–12, 14–15

Even in his unremitting sorrow and heartbreak, Job recognizes the power and mercy of God. That is the mark of a true worshipper!

Job, in the deepest part of his soul, knows that arguing with God holds a different motive than asking God sincere questions. Job is right—none of us is able to argue with God and expect to win. Yet the majestic truth remains that because Jesus is now our high priest and we are gloriously covered with His righteousness, we can boldly come into the throne room of the Most High God with our questions and with our concerns.

Therefore let us draw near with confidence to the throne of grace, so that we may receive mercy and find grace to help in time of need. —Hebrews 4:16

Thus, as believers in God, our dilemma is real and valid: we are dealing with storms that turn everything in our life upside down, and we are bewildered by them. At the same time, we have a passionate, nearly desperate, longing for the God who makes everything right—yet we can't understand how He is working in our lives. And so, in faith and in love, we continue to pray above the wind, to worship in the downpour, and to bow down in the midst of the devastation that the storm has created. And we *lean*—we lean on His great mercy and not on our own understanding. (See Proverbs 3:5.)

The Rest of My Little Story

I want to return to the story of the e-mail I received from a college acquaintance after I had been diagnosed with cancer. Remember how she suggested I had unforgiveness in my heart, and that is why I had been stricken with cancer? Well, after I quickly forgave her so I wouldn't become guilty of the sin she had accused me of, do you know what I did? I wrote her back an e-mail with these words:

Dear Sarah,[5]

Thanks for your e-mail and thanks especially for your prayers. I can certainly use them. God is good and I fully expect to come through this fire refined and filled with His joy.

In the meantime—know that it is always good to hear from you and that I treasure our friendship. Praying for you and yours today.

Blessings and joy,
Carol

And then do you know what I did? I deleted her original e-mail because I didn't want any reminder of the false accusation. I simply decided to bless her in Jesus's name.

---

5. Not her real name.

As we will see, Job ended up doing something every similar with the false accusations of his friends.

"Faith does not eliminate questions. But faith knows where to take them."

—Elisabeth Elliot

TWENTY

Worship While You Wait

Job was a servant of God who had been forced to choose how he would wait out the storm that was violently blowing in his direction. We all must choose exactly what will occupy our time and attention when we are in the dreaded position of waiting out a storm. What you decide to do during a tempest that has the audacity to damage your life is one of the most important choices you will ever make. If, during the storm, you can choose to worship rather than blame, your life might be even more triumphant in the post-storm period.

Job is not the only biblical character who had to make this particular decision. Abraham had to choose how to wait for God's promise of a son. Hannah had to choose how to wait during years of infertility. David had to choose how to wait when he was dealing with depression and loneliness. Esther had to choose how to wait for God's miraculous intervention to spare the lives of His people. Paul and Silas had to choose how to wait while they were in the depth and darkness of a Roman prison. What all of these biblical heroes and heroines have in common is not the fact that they faced a storm, but it is their resilient choice to *worship* in the midst of it. Earlier in this book, we have noted the same response by other biblical figures who were caught up in a tempest—it is universally the best response we can make.

"As for Me"

Job the blameless speaks on behalf of all of us as he declares his genuine worship to the Lord, his Maker. He speaks in faith as the boils continue to fester on his skin, his friends continue to antagonize, and the grief in his heart refuses to subside. Job declares what he knows to be the verifiable and immovable truth in the deepest part of himself:

As for me, I know that my Redeemer lives, and at the last He will take His stand on the earth. Even after my skin is destroyed, yet from my flesh I shall see God; whom I myself shall behold, and whom my eyes will see and not another. —Job 19:25–27

Each one of us must have a similar Job-like moment in the middle of the blast that has uprooted everything we have valued. We all must decide what theology we will embrace and what ultimate truths we will speak during the days of pain, torment, and ashes. Who your parents are doesn't determine your choice. Your spouse cannot decide this for you. Even your pastor is unable to make this determination on your behalf. This decision is solely between you and God. You must decide what to believe, what to speak, and how to behave at the darkest hour of your life.

The words you choose to utter while facing such a tempest reveal the degree of your intimacy with God. The declarations you make while the tornado is whirling around you reveal what you *know* about who He really is.

"As for me—I believe that God is good!"

"As for me—I will worship Him even in the deluge!"

"As for me—I will bless Him and never blame Him!"

"As for me—I will trust Him when everyone else accuses Him!"

"As for me…!"

I challenge you, even as you read these words, to declare God's goodness over your sharp disappointments and dashed dreams. I dare you to continue to worship the Lord even when you don't understand Him and when others around you are wailing. I call on you to bless His name even when your emotions are in torment. I urge you to put all of your hope in your good, good Father, regardless of what others are saying about your situation.

Job's words are especially powerful when you consider that his "friends" continued to blame him. Job was resolute, and he may have looked with pity upon the three men and their heart issues. The implication in his declaration from Job 19:25–27 is that his friends did not have the authority to speak on his behalf.

I can just picture Job pulling himself to his feet, in spite of the oozing, infected boils, and lifting his hands toward heaven while declaring, *"As for me…"*! It was Job's finest hour, and it can be your finest hour, too, when you make the same choice he did.

The Benefit and Deficit List

Job's choice to worship in spite of peer pressure, in spite of physical pain, in spite of financial ruin, and in spite of a future that had been stolen from him was an uncommon and determined choice. Choosing to worship, no matter what your circumstances may be, is never an easy or obvious decision; it takes great resolve and even greater discipline. Worship is a peculiar decision—but a holy one—when all you see is devastation across the horizon of your life Worship is the singular decision to keep your eyes on the Lord and not on your circumstances.

The prophet Isaiah, who lived many years after Job, spoke these powerful words concerning the remarkable choice to worship when others are weeping:

To grant those who mourn in Zion, giving them a garland instead of ashes, the oil of gladness instead of mourning, the mantle ["garment" NKJV, ASV] of praise instead of a spirit of fainting. So they will be called oaks of righteousness, the planting of the LORD, that He may be glorified. —Isaiah 61:3

I love making lists, and apparently so did the prophet Isaiah! The making and maintaining of lists has always helped me to manage my life as stress-free as possible. On any given day, I might be checking off items on my "To Do List" or sending cards to people on my "Need Encouragement List." I clean my home in an organized fashion due to my "Weekly House Cleaning List," and I remember everyone's birthday in our very large family because I took the time to make a "Family Birthday List."

Isaiah's beautiful list includes the benefits of worship—and the deficits of choosing not to worship. In Isaiah 61:3, *"Zion"* is symbolic of a place of high worship. The word *Zion* essentially means fortification, high place, or monument. The term *Zion* is used in Scripture to describe both the original city of David and the city of Jerusalem. Additionally, it can have other spiritual meanings. "Zion" can refer to the spiritual place of taking your pain to God and of remaining in His presence, where there is joy.

Isaiah, a man of boldness and insight, declares that when a believer takes their sorrow and mourning right into the presence of the Lord—to His "high place"—there will be an incredible and miraculous exchange that takes place due to that choice. According to Isaiah, if you will do that—if you will take your sorrow to the high place of worship—this is what you will receive:

1. You will be given a *"garland,"* or a crown. The garland that you receive as you offer your tears in a song of worship to the Lord represents the precious evidence that you are royalty, a child of the King!

2. You will receive the *"oil of gladness."* The oil of gladness symbolizes the bounty of joy that comes from a time of grand celebration. In the ancient Hebrew world, this type of oil was used only at banquets and

jubilant feasts. When you choose to worship rather than whine, you will be given the exquisite and extremely valuable commodity of joy! What wealth, indeed!

3. You will be given the *"mantle of praise,"* or a garment that a member of the choir was given to wear. Isaiah promises that you will be identified as a member of the choir who sings praises to God in public places. You will be given the job description of openly singing the attributes of God. Your pain will no longer alienate you but will give you a platform for all to see and hear!

Don't you just love those benefits? To receive them, who wouldn't want to worship the Lord at their worst moment in life? Who wouldn't want to sing above the storm? Who wouldn't want to praise God even while the tears were rolling down their cheeks?

However, if you read this verse closely, you will also discover the deficit list. If you choose not to worship while you grieve, you will remain in these very sad conditions:

1. You will continue to be identified as one who wears *"ashes,"* or who is in a perpetual state of mourning throughout their life.

2. You will continue to "mourn" with a wailing cry that is loud and shrill. Others will identify you not as a member of the choir but as one who has taken on the job description of a professional mourner.

3. You will be the victim of *"a spirit of fainting,"* which denotes something that is failing, a wick that is being extinguished, or eyes that are going blind. You will live in a weakened condition.

Which list would you like to identify your life? You will reflect the gifts or characteristics of the list you choose. If you choose to worship in the storm, you will receive all the benefits. If you decide to wail during the storm, you will retain all the deficits.

It is clear that feelings should never determine our capacity for worship. Even though we might feel like wailing, even though we might feel like one who is in perpetual mourning, and even though we might feel like our wick is quickly extinguishing, we, too, can declare with Job,

I know that my Redeemer lives, and at the last He will take His stand on the earth. —Job 19:25

Never Alone

One of the lies the enemy utters to a storm-tossed believer is that he or she is alone...abysmally forgotten and alone. The deceiver endeavors to convince a man or woman of God that no one has ever experienced their particular pain and that there is no one alive who is capable of understanding what they are going through. Accordingly, whenever you are in a storm, firmly remind yourself that you are not alone! You are in the excellent company of Abraham, Job, Hannah, David, Esther, and Paul and Silas. Generations of believers who came before you had to make this choice, and the generations who follow after you will look to you as their example—so sing loudly and extravagantly! Let no storm ever out-shout you!

"Choices will continually be necessary and—let us not forget—possible. Obedience to God is always possible. It is a deadly error to fall into the notion that when feelings are extremely strong we can do nothing but act on them."

—Elisabeth Elliot

TWENTY-ONE

The Rest of Job's Story...
Can Be the Rest of Your Story

Once upon a time, in the land of Uz, there was a righteous and blameless man whose name was Job. Satan decided to target this man, and God gave him permission to do so. In a single day, Job lost everything he had worked his entire life to gain. Disaster after disaster struck this innocent man with unmatched ferocity. His children were killed, his possessions and wealth were destroyed, his wife told him to *"curse God and die!"* (Job 2:9), and he was alone in his suffering—yet he continued to trust God.

Nevertheless, Satan had additional diabolical plans for Job and asked God's permission to attack him even further. God gave His consent because He had such great faith in the character of His servant. So Satan smote Job with painful, oozing boils all over his body. The enemy probably believed that would be the last straw for Job.

Pure Gold

What Satan had failed to take into consideration was that while this storm might have been the worst experience of Job's life, it would usher in his finest hour! After Job's foolish friends attacked him verbally, accusing him of having sinned against God and being the cause of his own troubles, Job reminded them that God was not finished with him yet. The end of Job's story would not entail his sitting in human pain and rubbing ashes all over his body. The stories of God's people never end in ashes but always with pure gold.

But He knows the way I take; when He has tried me, I shall come forth as gold. My foot has held fast to His path; I have kept His way and not turned aside. I have not departed from the command of His lips; I have treasured the words of His mouth more than my necessary food. —Job 23:10–12

Job's declaration reveals the purity and steadfastness of his heart. In the midst of intense personal pain, he understands that he is in the middle of a process of refinement from God. He knows that God's process will always, always, produce gold.

Job tells his friends, in effect, that he has not been listening to them the entire time they have been spouting their erroneous opinions, but that he has been listening to the voice of God! He communicates with these difficult comrades that they have not been speaking on God's behalf. Similarly, if your life has been the target of a massive and unwarranted blast of circumstances, listen for the voice of God in the middle of the wind and the rain. Other voices may try to minimize God's power and even blame Him for the havoc that has come your way, but don't listen to them. Listen for the voice of God calling you forth as pure gold!

God Speaks

Finally—in the midst of Job's human pain and his friends' pontifications—the Lord speaks! The God of the universe has been watching Job's life and listening to his conversations. I have often wondered if God would have spoken earlier had He been given the chance! Instead, human beings futilely tried to give their best answers—and failed. Into their ridiculous assumptions and foolish replies, God speaks:

Then the LORD answered Job out of the whirlwind and said, "Who is this that darkens counsel by words without knowledge?"

—Job 38:1–2

Jehovah, the holy God, comes to His own defense and begins His divine soliloquy. The following words from the Lord to Job never fail to bring a smile to my mouth and a giggle to my heart:

Now gird up your loins like a man, and I will ask you, and you instruct Me!   *—Job 38:3*

Do you see the humor in God's demand? He was saying, "Job—man up! Put on your big-boy pants!" What an interesting and droll way for the Lord to tell Job it was time for him to grow up and understand exactly who God is and what He is capable of doing on behalf of His children.

The next two chapters of the book of Job consist entirely of God questioning Job; we are presented with sixty-seven pointed verses in which God Almighty puts humanity in its proper place. Let's listen in on just two of the points He makes:

Where were you when I laid the foundation of the earth? Tell Me, if you have understanding, who set its measurements? Since you know. Or who stretched the line on it? On what were its bases sunk? Or who laid its cornerstone, when the morning stars sang together and all the sons of God shouted for joy?   *—Job 38:4–7*

Or who enclosed the sea with doors when, bursting forth, it went out from the womb; when I made a cloud its garment and thick

darkness its swaddling band, and I placed boundaries on it and
set a bolt and doors, and I said, "Thus far you shall come, but no
farther; and here shall your proud waves stop"? —Job 38:8–11

The Father concludes His grand inquisition by demanding an answer
from His servant:

Then the LORD *said to Job, "Will the faultfinder contend with the*
Almighty? Let him who reproves God answer it." —Job 40:1–2

In effect, God was saying to the storm-tossed man, "Job, if you have
something to say, say it now!" Then Job humbly and meekly responds to
His Creator:

Behold, I am insignificant; what can I reply to You? I lay my hand
on my mouth. Once I have spoken, and I will not answer; even
twice, and I will add nothing more. —Job 40:3–5

Job realizes that he has said too much, so he apologetically states that he
would add nothing more to the conversation with God but would only put
his hand over his mouth. What great advice—advice that ricochets through
the centuries to our lives today! Put your hand over your mouth and only
remove it if you are going to bless God in the middle of your storm!

Throughout the subsequent two chapters of Job, God continues to
remind His servant of His power and wisdom. At the end of this tragic
storm experience, the Lord wants Job to be reminded of His authority and
complete control over the world He has made. God wants Job to be in awe
of the fact that he has been invited to participate in such a wonderful world
with His Creator!

Are you in awe of what God has provided for you? Are you struck with
genuine wonder when you consider that you, like Job, are invited to participate in the universe that your Father has given to you? Even with all of its

flaws and failures, it truly is a wonderful world that we have been given the opportunity to live in.

I Take It Back!

I picture Job sitting there in the ruins of his life, with his three disgraceful companions inching away from him in humiliation. God has spoken—and the earth, and all who live in it, are now silent. Perhaps the silence is awkward for a minute or two, but then Job lifts up his head and responds to the call of heaven. His reply is so poignant and lovely that it is almost painful:

Then Job answered the LORD and said, "I know that You can do all things, and that no purpose of Yours can be thwarted. 'Who is this that hides counsel without knowledge?' Therefore I have declared that which I did not understand, things too wonderful for me, which I did not know. 'Hear, now, and I will speak; I will ask You, and You instruct me.' I have heard of You by the hearing of the ear; but now my eye sees You; therefore I retract, and I repent in dust and ashes." —Job 42:1–6

The refining work in Job's life is complete! He retracts all that he has spoken out of pain, out of selfish questions, and out of understandable human emotions. Job is emerging from his personal storm as pure gold because God has completed a work in his heart so vast that he is able to retract and repent. Job speaks plainly and powerfully to the One whom he serves. When he expresses, *"I know that You can do all things, and that no purpose of Yours can be thwarted,"* what he is essentially stating is, "Not my will, Father, but Your will, be done in my life." (See Luke 22:42.) Job has laid his earthly agenda down and is ready to partner with his Father in heaven for the remainder of his days.

Someone Is Listening

God was not going to let Eliphaz, Bildad, and Zophar slink away quietly, because He had been listening to their conversation with Job. Job's friends were utterly clueless when it came to the things of God the Father. The Lord had noted their ignorance and had heard their accusations and cruel words, and He had a thing or two to say to these three stooges!

It came about after the LORD had spoken these words to Job, that the LORD said to Eliphaz the Temanite, "My wrath is kindled against you and against your two friends, because you have not spoken of Me what is right as My servant Job has. Now therefore, take for yourselves seven bulls and seven rams, and go to My servant Job, and offer up a burnt offering for yourselves, and My servant Job will pray for you. For I will accept him so that I may not do with you according to your folly, because you have not spoken of Me what is right, as My servant Job has." So Eliphaz the Temanite and Bildad the Shuhite and Zophar the Naamathite went and did as the LORD told them; and the LORD accepted Job.

—Job 42:7–9

These are exceedingly sobering verses for anyone who loves to give advice to those who are going through a difficult time in life. Someone is listening to every word that you speak, and His name is God. Don't mistakenly believe that you are going to get away with spewing verbal vomit on someone who is in dire personal misery.

Do not be hasty in word or impulsive in thought to bring up a matter in the presence of God. For God is in heaven and you are on the earth; therefore let your words be few. —Ecclesiastes 5:2

But I tell you that every careless word that people speak, they shall give an accounting for it in the day of judgment.

—Matthew 12:36

The Power of Prayer

When Job prayed for his friends, God accepted his prayer and forgave them. Remember, *"the effective prayer of a righteous man can accomplish much"* (James 5:16). And then a miracle occurred! All that had been ravaged was returned to Job *"twofold"*:

> The LORD restored the fortunes of Job when he prayed for his friends, and the LORD increased all that Job had twofold. Then all his brothers and all his sisters and all who had known him before came to him, and they ate bread with him in his house; and they consoled him and comforted him for all the adversities that the LORD had brought on him. And each one gave him one piece of money, and each a ring of gold.   —Job 42:10–11

Job experienced the bestowal of a double blessing because he obeyed the Lord and because he prayed for those who had carelessly and needlessly hurt him.

The Rest Is the Best

> The LORD blessed the latter days of Job more than his beginning; and he had 14,000 sheep and 6,000 camels and 1,000 yoke of oxen and 1,000 female donkeys.   —Job 42:12

If you reread Job 1:3, you will be reminded that in the beginning, Job possessed *"7,000 sheep, 3,000 camels, 500 yoke of oxen, 500 female donkeys."* Once more we see that the blessing of restoration God gave to Job in the final period of his life was exactly twice what he had enjoyed at the beginning of the story.

The Lord blessed Job even more than He had previously. This is what God will do for men and women who continually declare His wisdom and power even while they are struggling in inclement conditions. This is also what God will do for men and women who will repent.

If you can practice the "Job Principle" and worship even while you are grieving, the Lord will bless your life beyond measure as well. If you will pray for those who have hurt you, if you will bless even those who have persecuted you, the Lord will take care of you! He will not only restore your reputation and your loss, but He will also increase all that you have! God, our Creator and Father, takes great joy in giving to His children a double blessing of favor, honor, and heritage.

And now we come to one of the most beautiful passages about restoration in the entire Bible. Every time I read these five closing verses of the book of Job, my heart melts within me and tears of joy begin to spill out of the corners of my eyes.

[Job] *had seven sons and three daughters. He named the first Jemimah, and the second Keziah, and the third Keren-happuch. In all the land no women were found so fair as Job's daughters; and their father gave them inheritance among their brothers. After this, Job lived 140 years, and saw his sons and his grandsons, four generations. And Job died, an old man and full of days.*

—Job 42:13–17

One of the most delightful aspects of these final verses is that we are told the names of Job's daughters. This was in a historical period when men were considered to be everything and women were thought to have little value. Yet Job viewed his daughters as significant and beautiful. Their names are included for all generations to read. *Women matter.* They mattered in the family of Job and they matter in the family of God. Do not allow any storm in life to rob you of your significance to the kingdom and to the economy of God. Job gave his daughters an inheritance; and God, the greatest Father in all of eternity, has given His daughters an inheritance as well!

"Job died, an old man and full of days." Job wasn't filled with pain or regret; he was filled with life! His final days were overflowing with the wonderful things that living life for the Father always delivers. This, my friend, is a better ending than "happily ever after"! Having your life filled with the blessings of God is the grandest finale indeed!

"He remembers our frame and knows that we are dust. He may sometimes chasten us, it is true, but even this He does with a smile, the proud, tender smile of a Father who is bursting with pleasure over an imperfect but promising son who is coming every day to look more and more like the One whose child he is."

—A. W. Tozer

PART SIX

Speak to the Storm

TWENTY-TWO

A Biggie!

I have a secret belief that Jesus loved the beach—and so do I! I am a sun-drenched girl who would rather have a bevy of freckles on her nose and a healthy tan than a perfect, pale complexion any day of the week and any season of any year. I have a sweet suspicion that Jesus sported bronzed skin due to His days spent walking along the sandy shores of the Sea of Galilee.

Because of my love for the beach, I particularly delight in reading biblical stories about Jesus at the seashore—even the storm stories! One such account is told in three of the four gospels. Matthew, Mark, and Luke all tell of a ferocious gale that blew up quickly on the Sea of Galilee one fine day. Since this storm is referenced in three of the Gospels, we will be looking at all three accounts of the gale and then comparing the points of view from which they were told. (Remember that this storm *preceded* the tempest we studied at the beginning of this book, during which Peter walked on the water to Jesus.)

The storm that only Jesus had the power to control was a disturbance that some translations actually describe as having been caused by an earthquake. Therefore, this was not a gentle spring shower or even a tropical thundershower—it was the ultimate monster of a storm.

Not a Cloud in the Sky!

The Sea of Galilee, also known as Lake Gennesaret, is located in a basin and is surrounded by mountains. Although the sea (actually a lake) is relatively small in circumference (thirteen miles long, seven miles wide), it is startlingly deep, descending to a hundred and fifty feet in some places. Another interesting fact about this lake is that the shoreline is six hundred and eighty feet below sea level.

This particular sea basin is geographically famous for being susceptible to sudden, violent storms. When cool air from the Mediterranean is drawn through the narrow mountain passes, it mixes with the hot, humid air over the lake. The spaces between the mountains serve as funnels for great blasts of cool wind, which cause this fairly small body of water to become suddenly tempestuous. This often results in violent instability in the weather patterns. Many a fishing vessel has ended up on the bottom of the sea due to these giant squalls. At times, the waves on this small lake have been measured to be as high as twenty feet. One seasoned traveler described the surface of the Sea of Galilee during a storm as a "huge boiling caldron."[6]

Let's now begin to look at our storm story from the viewpoints of the three gospels.

Now on one of those days Jesus and His disciples got into a boat, and He said to them, "Let us go over to the other side of the lake." So they launched out. —Luke 8:22

---

6. See John Ross McDuff, *The Footsteps of St. Peter* (New York: Robert Carter and Brothers, 1876), 95–96, footnote 1, https://books.google.com/books?id=cBdFAAAAYAAJ&pg=PA95&lpg=PA95&dq=sea+of+galilee+huge+boiling+caldron.

On that day, when evening came, [Jesus] said to them, "Let us go over to the other side." Leaving the crowd, they took Him along with them in the boat, just as He was; and others boats were with Him. —Mark 4:35–36

When [Jesus] got into the boat, His disciples followed Him. —Matthew 8:23

———————

It was early evening, and Jesus suggested to His disciples that they take a boat ride on the Sea of Galilee. Everyone agreed to go with Him. These followers of Jesus, particularly Peter, could be an opinionated bunch, but no one offered any resistance to this evening voyage. Not one of the savvy seamen—Peter, Andrew, James, or John—found a worthy reason why this was not an excellent time to set sail on the Sea of Galilee. Evening was the best time for sailing on this unusual body of water because the storms that often blew across it came during the afternoon hours. Apparently, the lake was smooth and there was not a cloud in the sky! The disciples did not foolishly head into a storm; this was certainly not a tempest they saw coming.

Thus, there was no reason in the natural for these former fishermen and the rest of the disciples not to follow Jesus into the boat and across the sea. They trusted Him and were looking forward to the next great adventure with their Teacher and Friend.

I so often see myself in these young men who decided to follow Jesus; I can trust Him when the skies are sunny and when my life is at peace. I can willingly boast, "Jesus! I will go anywhere with You"—as long as I can see all the way to the other side of the shore. However, when the least little breeze of negative circumstances threatens my well-being, I suddenly wonder where Jesus is and if He knows the stormy conditions that are beginning to rock the waves of my innocent life.

The Basin of Fear

And behold, there arose a great storm ["tempest" NKJV, ASV] on the sea, so that the boat was being covered with the waves; but Jesus Himself was asleep. —Matthew 8:24

The Greek word translated here as *"storm"* or *"tempest"* is *seismos*, the same word used in the Bible for "earthquake." This word is used to communicate not only the violence of the storm, but also its probable cause. Many Bible historians believe that this brutal monsoon might actually have been instigated by some sort of tremor in the earth's surface, which then caused instability in the water. When the waves in the Sea of Galilee began to rock destructively due to a fault in the earth's surface, likely there was a storm brewing in the atmosphere as well. It was the "perfect storm," where the forces of nature joined together to create havoc, fear—and damage.

And there arose a fierce gale of wind, and the waves were breaking over the boat so much that the boat was already filling up.
—Mark 4:37

We've just read this verse as a historical record; now let's read it in a personal context. Can you imagine what was going on in the hearts of these young men? Their boat, which was being fiercely rocked by the cataclysmic power of nature, was filling up with water! They had to hang on to the mast or to anything that was tied down on the boat in order not to be washed overboard, and yet they also desperately needed to bail out the water that was threatening to sink their ship.

But as they were sailing along [Jesus] fell asleep; and a fierce gale of wind descended on the lake, and they began to be swamped and to be in danger. —Luke 8:23

Told from three different perspectives, the message is the same: the boat was being covered, literally swamped, by the high waves of the wicked storm. The words that are used in the Greek in all three verses communicate the fact that the boat was being filled to capacity with the water that the storm was churning up. The danger was great and their very lives were at stake. Their boat couldn't take one more drop of water or it would sink to the bottom of the Sea of Galilee—where other unfortunate mariners had gone before them.

The disciples had followed Jesus on this now treacherous journey, but He was asleep while they were waist-high in water! Have you ever been in a similar situation? You were certain that you heard the voice of the Lord leading you in a specific direction when suddenly you felt like you were being overcome by disappointment, challenging circumstances, and difficult people. Perhaps you felt that you couldn't take one more problem or you would drown in your stormy circumstances. You weren't sure whether to bail water or hang on for dear life in the midst of the quake that was rocking your very world. What is a sailor to do in such life-threatening conditions?

"Don't You Care?"

Jesus Himself was in the stern, asleep on the cushion; and they woke Him and said to Him, "Teacher, do You not care that we are perishing?" —Mark 4:38

The disciples were so overwhelmed by the storm and by the threat of death that they forgot who was with them! Jesus Himself was their Companion on the ship! However, as so often happens during a stormy season in life, they were more aware of their storm than they were of His presence.

Ouch! That reminder hurts, doesn't it? I have lost count of the times during my life when I have been more aware of my inclement circumstances than I have been of His presence. I have to repent in humility as I recall the situations in which I have panicked rather than prayed. I am ashamed of the moments when I have allowed my human fear to trump the faith I hold so dearly. When we give in to fear, it wipes out the power of our faith.

The disciples' despair was accelerated by circumstances that were out of their control. Although some of them were skilled fisherman and were accustomed to the storms that were birthed on this lake, their impassioned reaction causes us further reason to believe that this particular storm was incredibly severe.

When life stirs up an especially caustic blast of unstable conditions, we, like the twelve disciples, often forget the power of the God whom we serve. And in our weakest and most vulnerable moments, we, as did they, accuse our Lord of not caring about the storm that has interrupted our idyllic life.

Ouch! That hurts, too, doesn't it? I weep when I think that I have had the cruel bravado to accuse the Lord, whose very character is defined by the trait of "love" (see 1 John 4:8, 16), of not caring about me or my life conditions. He is with me—and He is with you! What comfort there should be in that knowledge! His presence is able to calm any storm and to save any water-saturated sailor!

In Good Hands

I find it striking that while the disciples were panicking, Jesus was sleeping. While the sea-savvy sailors were filled with fear, Jesus was filled with peace and contentment. Please note that the circumstances of Jesus and the circumstances of the disciples were exactly the same, but their reactions were completely opposite. In the middle of my storms, I want to be like Jesus—not like those who accused Him of not caring. I want to be able to sleep peacefully while the world rages around me, and I long to be a carrier of the peace and hope of His presence.

Jesus was able to sleep during those violent conditions because He intimately knew the Father—the One who created the seas and the wind. He knew that He was in very good hands even in the middle of a ferocious storm. And so are you, my friend. So are you.

"Never make a permanent decision based upon a temporary storm. No matter how raging the billows are today, remind yourself, 'This, too, shall pass.'"

—T. D. Jakes

TWENTY-THREE

Amazed—But Not Afraid

I was raised in a family that believed in the capacity of the local church to bring stability to a community and to enable its members to receive life-giving power. The ministry of the church was at the very center not only of our spiritual life, but also of our social life. It set our daily priorities and was a sovereign call to service.

My family was in attendance at the little Methodist church just down the street from my home every single time the doors were opened. Whether it was a weekly worship service, a prayer meeting, a revival service, or a Sunday school picnic, the Burton family was there—spit shined! We inevitably arrived early and were the last ones out the door. My mom played the organ, chose the hymns, and was in charge of the Women's Mission Union. My dad was the adult Sunday school teacher, often functioned as an assistant pastor—visiting the sick and preaching when the pastor was unable to—and in his loving and kind way brought peace to our little corner of the church world. As you can tell, our family was the living, breathing, show-and-tell of what it meant to be a "church family" in the twentieth century.

My dearest memories of being raised in the safety and joy of a country church were the song services. How the lyrics of those great hymns of faith impacted my view of God and what He was capable of doing! Their words have shaped my faith in an undeniable and compelling manner, and their influence in my life has continued to this very day.

I was first taught how to "stand on the promises of Christ my King" by belting out those words from a robust little heart. I committed to sincerely "trust and obey" through all the seasons of my life when I was but a mere wisp of a child. I became acquainted with my dearest lifetime Friend as I meaningfully sang, "What a Friend we have in Jesus."

Two lesser-known songs I remember singing have given me the faith and the courage to weather many a storm in my life. At the risk of being thought of as old-fashioned or even "archaic," I long to share the lyrics of these songs with those of you who are currently in a storm of great magnitude. So, before we carry on with the story of the boys in a boat on a storm-tossed sea, I encourage you to first read these few stanzas of a song that never goes out of style. When I was battling cancer, this is the song I often sang in the night; it echoed in my soul from when I was just a little girl learning to sing alto in the church choir:

Far away in the depths of my spirit tonight

Rolls a melody sweeter than psalm;

In celestial-like strains it unceasingly falls

O'er my soul like an infinite calm.

[Refrain:]

Peace, peace, wonderful peace,

Coming down from the Father above!

Sweep over my spirit forever, I pray

In fathomless billows of love!

What a treasure I have in this wonderful peace

Buried deep in the heart of my soul,

So secure that no power can mine it away

While the years of eternity roll!

[Refrain:]

Peace, peace, wonderful peace,

Coming down from the Father above!

Sweep over my spirit forever, I pray

In fathomless billows of love!

I am resting tonight in this wonderful peace,

Resting sweetly in Jesus' control;

For I'm kept from all danger by night and by day

And His glory is flooding my soul!

[Refrain:]

Peace, peace, wonderful peace,

Coming down from the Father above!

Sweep over my spirit forever, I pray

In fathomless billows of love![7]

Can we travel back through time for just one more song from my childhood? I guarantee that the refrain from this song will serve as a victorious

7. W. D. Cornell, "Wonderful Peace," 1889.

reminder for you, through all of the storms in your life, that there is an unseen power at work that is greater than any storm you are in!

> Wonderful the matchless grace of Jesus,
>
> Deeper than the mighty rolling sea;
>
> Wonderful grace, all sufficient for me, for even me;
>
> Broader than the scope of my transgressions,
>
> Greater far than all my sin and shame;
>
> O magnify the precious name of Jesus,
>
> Praise His name![8]

Did you hear them? Did you hear, joining with you, the voices of the "sailors" of past ages singing above the waves of your storm this very day? Their song is not old-fashioned, nor is it archaic; it is timeless as it calls you to a place of wonderful peace even in the middle of your storm!

"Lord, Save Us!"

And they came to Him and woke Him, saying, "Save us, Lord; we are perishing!" —Matthew 8:25

We know that the disciples had witnessed many miracles by Jesus, yet they were still filled with fear in this particular storm. We also know that at least four of these young men were experienced sailors and certainly had encountered blasts of wind and rain in their lives; however they were alarmed because they were unaware that Jesus was able to control even this situation in their lives.

This is a powerful reminder for all of us who find ourselves in agitated circumstances that Jesus is willing to help us if we will just ask Him. We

---

8. Haldor Lillenas, "Wonderful Grace of Jesus," 1918.

should never underestimate His power and grace, even during the most unstable days in life.

You may believe (falsely) that your life is about to be swept overboard by the danger and cruelty of an unexpected storm. Rather than embrace fear, cry out to God and ask Him to save you! Rather than accusing Him of not caring, wouldn't it be advantageous to ask the Lord, who created you, to deliver you from the cutting winds of circumstances and from the rising waters of difficulties? Instead of giving in to fear, why not use every bit of your remaining strength to call out to the Father in your time of distress and discomfort?

And they came to Jesus and woke Him up, saying, "Master, Master, we are perishing!" And He got up and rebuked the wind and the surging waves, and they stopped, and it became calm.

—Luke 8:24

When you call on Jesus in the middle of your raging monsoon, He will indeed come to your rescue simply because He cares about you. How He loves to hear the voice of a waterlogged sailor crying out to Him for help! He was asleep in this storm-tossed boat because He was at peace; it wasn't because He didn't care about His disciples. All that these panic-stricken nautical geniuses had to do was call on the name of the Lord—and that is all you have to do as well. When you cry out to Him in a time of need, He will hear your voice and calm your storm. It's what He does best!

Wonderful Peace!

And He got up and rebuked the wind and said to the sea, "Hush, be still." And the wind died down and it became perfectly calm.

—Mark 4:39

What had been violent was now *"perfectly calm"*; what had formerly threatened to destroy the disciples now became a place of peace. How did this happen? It happened because Jesus was in the boat! Jesus has always had authority over His creation; every element that was made by Him is subject to Him. Accordingly, He is in charge of your life, and your circumstances will never have the last word in a storm when you cry out to the One who created you. The voice of Jesus is authoritatively able to calm any storm you are in today. Simply call to Him, and He will respond.

> *He said to them, "Why are you afraid, you men of little faith?" Then He got up and rebuked the winds and the sea, and it became perfectly calm.* —Matthew 8:26

Here in Matthew's account of this storm story, we see again that after a word from the Master, the violent explosion of hurricane-like winds, relentless torrents of rain, and unremitting waves became instantly and completely calm as far as the eye could see.

The Greek word translated *"afraid"* in this verse is *deiloi*, which means cowardly fear. These miracle-saturated disciples should have been exhibiting faith rather than acting like scaredy-cats. We cannot allow fear to steal from us our awareness of the presence of our loving Savior. We cannot allow fear to rob from us what the Lord is able to do for us. We cannot allow fear to skew our view of what is actually happening in our life.

Jesus confronted His waterlogged sailors about their lack of faith. He longed for them to trust Him even during the most savage days of life. If you have set your heart on being a disciple of Jesus Christ, then you, too, must confront your issues of fear. You must determine that even when you are in circumstances that you don't understand and never would have chosen, you will continue to trust Him!

Nothing Short of Amazing

> *And He said to them, "Where is your faith?" They were fearful and amazed, saying to one another, "Who then is this, that He*

commands even the winds and the water, and they obey Him?"

—Luke 8:25

Those who had been afraid were now amazed and filled with a reverent fear because of what Jesus had done. Their "yellow-bellied" fear was now eclipsed by their utter wonder over the power and authority of the One who had been sleeping on a pillow in the stern of the boat just a few minutes earlier. The disciples were unable to mask the divine awe that had come alive in them. Awe is our proper response to the One who can control the wildest elements of creation.

Can you picture this scenario? Jesus stood up boldly in the stern of a boat that was being tossed to and fro by twenty-foot waves. He had supreme confidence in His calling and in His authority over creation. According to the account in Mark 4:39, it took only three words from the Master—*"Hush, be still"*—and the wind immediately submitted and the waves instantly obeyed.

And He said to them, "Why are you afraid? Do you still have no faith?" They became very much afraid and said to one another, "Who then is this, that even the wind and the sea obey Him?"

—Mark 4:40–41

The men were amazed, and said, "What kind of a man is this, that even the winds and the sea obey Him?" —Matthew 8:27

At this point, the disciples were just shaking their heads at one another and saying, "Did you just see what I saw? What just happened to us!"

Perhaps, drenched in salt water and seaweed, Thomas turned to Peter and said, "I don't believe it, do you?" To which Peter might have replied, "He must be the Son of the living God! He must be!"

And I wonder, I just wonder, if a tear coursed down the cheek of the compassionate John as he checked on everyone to make sure they were all okay.

The Last Word

When you find yourself in the middle of a vicious, cruel storm, remind yourself that Jesus is at peace. He is not surprised by the tempest that threatens to drown you. He is in full control of the wild blast even while you are in the middle of it. If Jesus is at rest, then you should be too; if Jesus can sleep through storms, then you should be able to as well. Your deepest calling in life is to be like Jesus—even in the midst of adverse and tormenting conditions.

Jesus is still the Master of creation, and He is with you. Don't allow the storm to stir up fear within you and swallow your faith. Resolve this day that every storm that gathers on the horizon of your life will reveal to the world that Jesus is in your boat! And never forget that where Jesus is, there is always perfect peace. You are not alone in the storm; you are in the company of the One who is well able to control what is happening around you. There will be times and seasons in your life when there is no one but Jesus who has the power to do anything to help you. Perhaps you are in such a season today. If you are, remind yourself emphatically that God is in control!

Jesus wants you to be brave even when your world is in turmoil; He longs for you to exhibit faith when everyone else believes you have a reason to cower in fear. As disciples of Jesus, our faith is always tested by the storms of life and by the challenges that inevitably and suddenly arise. Yet if the elements of nature are subject to the command of Jesus, then the situations of your life are under His authority as well.

God, after He spoke long ago to the fathers in the prophets in many portions and in many ways, in these last days has spoken to us in His Son, whom He appointed heir of all things, through whom also He made the world. And He is the radiance of His

*glory and the exact representation of His nature, and **upholds all
things by the word of His power.*** —Hebrews 1:1–3

Jesus is upholding your life *"by the word of His power"*! Don't make the same mistake the disciples made and doubt in the storm what you believed in the sunshine. In the will of God for your life, there is no situation and there is no storm where His presence cannot be accessed and where His words will not make a remarkable difference!

"Sometimes God calms the storm but always
He calms His child."

—Author unknown

PART SEVEN

The Aftermath

TWENTY-FOUR

Listen and Obey!

Shortly after their marriage, a young couple wished to buy a home, and while they didn't have a lot of money, they were overflowing with energy and creative ideas. These newlyweds knew that a fixer-upper was all they could afford, and so, after much research, they found the top realtor in town. With this successful and respected businesswoman guiding their search, they started the hunt for their dream home.

Day after day, the eager young couple met the realtor at homes in various neighborhoods. They examined every run-down, vacant house in town, looking at the seals on the windows, the size of the rooms, the condition of the cabinetry, and the state of the bathrooms. These savvy and opinionated young adults, very sure of their priorities, were intent on not compromising even the smallest desire of their hearts for their new home.

The realtor they had selected was the total picture of success: she always dressed in a designer suit with coordinating shoes and brandished an expensive handbag. Each time, after the couple enthusiastically perused a home, this realtor would quietly lay her purse on the dilapidated front porch or broken steps and then crawl under the house. And each time, without any fanfare or emotion, she would methodically declare, while wiping the dirt from her expensive suit, "No, I won't let you buy this house."

The young couple always had the same response—they were gobsmacked! They would stand by incredulously as the realtor marched back to her expensive car, ready to move on to the next home.

"This Is It!"

Finally, the weeks of house hunting became months, and the couple's working relationship with the realtor became tenuous. Then, the realtor invited the young couple to see a house that was a true monstrosity. It was a rodent-laden, century-old home that had stood uninhabited for nearly half of those years. The couple tried to think of a tactful way to fire the realtor, whom they thought had lost her very successful mind. But the experienced realtor quietly climbed under the home, as was her custom. This time, as she crawled out again, she said with great joy, "This is it! This is the home for you!"

You see, this realtor knew a secret that the young couple was not yet aware of. She understood that when buying a home, *it is all about the foundation.* The quality of the foundation determines the stability of the house during all kinds of environmental conditions and temperature variations. It affects the solidity of the walls as well as the settling of the floorboards and whether the house will crumble over time. It is the foundation that makes all the difference in a home's overall durability and value. Unfortunately, most of us focus on the visual aspects of our homes rather than on the strength of its unseen foundation.

This is true not only of the brick, stone, or wooden homes in which we live but also of our physical and spiritual "homes"—our very lives. What you have the capacity to become depends upon your foundation. Moreover, whether you will have the tenacity to endure the storms of life depends entirely upon that foundation.

By wisdom a house is built, and by understanding it is established.
                                                    —Proverbs 24:3

A Carpenter's Perspective

To help us internalize this vital truth, for our final storm story, we will examine a symbolic tempest from one of Jesus's parables. In order to hear this story, we must join Jesus in Capernaum, a fishing village near the Sea of Galilee. Jesus has positioned Himself on a mountain on the north shore of this well-known body of water, and He has just concluded what is known as "The Sermon on the Mount." Even among secular scholars, there is a general agreement that this particular sermon is perhaps the greatest moral discourse ever uttered. Here are Jesus's closing words:

> *Therefore everyone who hears these words of Mine and acts on them, may be compared to a wise man who built his house on the rock. And the rain fell, and the floods came, and the winds blew and slammed against that house; and yet it did not fall, for it had been founded on the rock. Everyone who hears these words of Mine and does not act on them, will be like a foolish man who built his house on the sand. The rain fell, and the floods came, and the winds blew and slammed against that house; and it fell—and great was its fall.* —Matthew 7:24–27

I have always wondered if, as Jesus looked out across the landscape of the shoreline, He actually saw a home that had been built upon the sand, one that had been battered by the winds and waves of a recent squall. Maybe the house was now uninhabitable due to the damage it had sustained—because it had no solid foundation. I also wonder if Jesus had within His range of sight a less impressive house that, although it had taken hits from the same powerful storm, was standing solid and strong—because its foundation had been built upon rock.

The fact that Jesus told a parable in which He compared two different builders and two different types of locations is not surprising. Most people are apt to talk from the perspective of their personal experiences and knowledge. Jesus was raised by Mary and by Joseph, who was a carpenter. Additionally, Jesus was apparently in charge of the family business before He began His public ministry when He was about thirty years old, so He knew the trade. I imagine that His hands were scarred in places where splinters had dug deeply under His skin. Some of His fingernails might have been battered from a hammer hit or two. However, it was His head knowledge of the intricacies of carpentry and what it takes to construct a stable, sturdy structure that came to light in the words He spoke and the story He told.

Jesus shared from His experience and knowledge as a Man and as a carpenter. He was aware of the fact that both wise and foolish people build houses. He also knew that the difference between the homes of the wise and those of the foolish had much to do with what type of land their homes were built upon. A home that costs ten million dollars today but is built on sand might not last through one major storm, whereas a home that costs only a hundred thousand dollars but is built on rock might last for generations through many great storms.

Hearing—and Acting

As you have probably already ascertained from reading this short, yet powerful, parable, the houses Jesus was talking about represent people's lives. By now, we should have no doubt that emotional, spiritual, and mental tempests are sure to surround us and even threaten to destroy us. However, Jesus tells us how to make it through such storms without any permanent destruction to our lives. Moreover, His words give us a greater understanding of how to be *prepared* for these tempests.

The only way to make it through life's torrential rains and gusting winds is not merely to *hear* the words of Jesus—including all the truths found in Scripture—but also to *act* on them. Listening is only part of the Carpenter's equation; obeying is the most important aspect.

If you just read your Bible and never embrace its principles as your own, then, when the disturbances of life begin to arise on the horizon, you will be in no position to stand strong. If you simply listen to sermons based on God's Word and never apply their precepts to your own system of living, your foundation will crumble at the first roll of thunder. Neglecting to embrace the truths of Scripture as your standard for living is like remodeling your kitchen cabinets and painting the side of your house and believing these cosmetic changes have the power to save your home during the next tornado that comes your way.

However, if you desire to build the kind of life that will stand firm during illness, financial stress, family challenges, rejection, and failure, then you must not only read the Bible—you must "do" the Bible. You must not only hear the Word of God—you must obey the Word of God. You must not only go to church—you must become the church. That means being a receptive dwelling place for the Holy Spirit and allowing Him to work His grace and power in your life.

For we are God's fellow workers; you are God's field, God's building. According to the grace of God which was given to me, like a wise master builder I laid a foundation, and another is building on it. But each man must be careful how he builds on it. For no man can lay a foundation other than the one which is laid, which is Jesus Christ. —1 Corinthians 3:9–11

A Family Motto

As He concluded the Sermon on the Mount, Jesus told His disciples and the crowd that had gathered not merely to hear His words but also to act on them. When the apostle James, the half-brother of Jesus, wrote his epistle, he chose the same philosophy as one of his teaching themes:

But prove yourselves doers of the word, and not merely hearers who delude themselves. —James 1:22

The fact that both Jesus and James taught from this perspective causes me, a mother of five, to wonder if the admonition to both "hear and do" was something they had been taught in their family home by their mother, Mary. I know that each of the five McLeod kids, although they are now grown and living on their own, can recite nearly word for word some of the philosophies that were taught in *our* family home by Mama McLeod:

"Find your happy heart!"

"Trouble starts with fun!"

"If you whine, you won't get your way!"

"It's more important to be kind!"

"Listen and obey right away...all the way...in a happy way!"

"Delayed obedience is disobedience!"

Perhaps Mary—the mother of not only Jesus and James, but also a host of other children—had taught her progeny, "Don't just listen to my words...obey my words!" Whatever the case, Jesus and James were both wise men who knew the prudence of calling their audiences to both hearing and action.

The words and the heart of Jesus echo through the ages as He calls each one of us today to stormproof living. If you want to stand strong in spite of the blasts of circumstantial tempests, situational hurricanes, and relational blizzards, you will *listen* to the words of Jesus and then you will *act* on the words of Jesus. When you build a life based on that scriptural advice, you can be sure that your foundation will not be moved or shaken, no matter what adverse winds blow your way.

"God permits temptation because it does for us what the storms do for the oaks—it roots us; and what the fire does for the paintings on the porcelain—it makes them permanent."

—Mrs. Charles E. Cowman, *Streams in the Desert*

TWENTY-FIVE

Jaw-Dropping Amazement

If you long to be in the scriptural category known as "wise builder," you will incorporate biblical principles—including those found in the Bible's storm stories—into the very foundation of your life. Then, as you continue to build, you will assuredly make the sound decisions of a disciple of Jesus Christ who has been solidly established on the words and heart of the heavenly Father. Avoid making decisions based on your emotions or the opinions of popular culture. A wise builder selects building blocks that will add to the strength of the foundation, not weaken it.

The building blocks of your life should include biblical principles such as the following:

+ Be a fruit-bearing Christian, in all types of climate, even during days of drought—and especially during the storms of life.

+ Pray without ceasing. If you are breathing, continue to have a passionate and active prayer life. Never stop praying!

+ Be generous all the time.

+ Refuse to worry, even when there is tornadic activity around your life.

+ Share your faith with others and give the powerful report of how God has sheltered you even in the worst of life's storms.

+ Forgive those who have wronged you.

Everyone who hears these words of Mine and does not act on them, will be like a foolish man who built his house on the sand. The rain fell, and the floods came, and the winds blew and slammed against that house; and it fell—and great was its fall.

—Matthew 7:26–27

After Jesus presented the blueprint of how the wise person builds a life, He then revealed what the result of shoddy craftsmanship in one's life looks like. If you hear the words of Jesus by reading your Bible daily, but refuse to allow those words to change your heart, your decisions, and your habits, your life will be in the red zone of storm activity. It doesn't matter how "great" or how "expensive" your life may appear from the outside, what matters is that you have foolishly built a life on human philosophy or on self-centered living. The words of Jesus resound through the ages to the choices that we make even today. Can you hear Him? Can you hear Him cautioning you, *"Don't do it! Don't build your life on the whims of the culture! Don't make life-altering decisions based upon how you feel! Don't do it! Just don't do it!"*

The philosophies of humanity are sinking sand upon which to build a life. When the storms of life blow—and they will—your life will go splat! If you have built a life based upon opinions or preferences, when the cyclones of disaster head in your way—and they will—your life will splinter into thousands of broken pieces. When gusts of financial instability, health challenges, and personal rejection blow across the foundation of your life—and they will—you might as well yell, "Timber!" Earthly systems, political opinions, entertainment, and temporary pleasures have no power to protect your life when a tempest is headed your direction.

Amazed by Authority

The disciple Matthew shares an interesting piece of information concerning the crowd's response to Jesus after He concluded His Sermon on the Mount with the simple, yet meaningful, storm story we have just reviewed:

When Jesus had finished these words, the crowds were amazed at His teaching; for He was teaching them as one having authority, and not as their scribes. —Matthew 7:28–29

Even the elementary teaching of Jesus concerning the wise builder and the foolish builder stirred up life-changing amazement in the multitudes. They had never heard anything like it! This story was so full of power and dynamic principles that astonishment began to spread like wildfire among the crowd. When they compared the teaching of Jesus with the teaching of the religious leaders of their day, the juxtaposition was jaw-dropping!

Jesus had come with a message that was fresh yet authoritative; new but wise; simple yet rich. The disciples and the crowd that gathered on that particular day had just been instructed in a truth that could transform their daily lives. They not only needed to listen to the words of Jesus as interesting teaching—they had to base their lives on them. Because of this one simple, yet deep, lesson, their lives could now be stormproof.

"Finding God does not mean building a house in a land of no storms, but building a house that no storm can destroy."

—Author unknown

TWENTY-SIX

Singing in the Rain

So, tell me: When the waves of life begin to overwhelm you—and they will—what will you do? When the gusting winds of circumstances threaten to blow you off your chosen course—and they will—what will keep you moving in the right direction? When a blizzard of difficult situations and disappointments begins to freeze your very destiny—and it will—what choices will you make?

Shelter from the Storm

Throughout *StormProof*, we have battened down the hatches and ridden out many biblical tempests together. Along this journey, we have identified a number of ways by which we can prepare for life's storms and sustain ourselves during these tempests. They all point to the best possible answer to the above questions: run for Shelter! Run into the safety and comfort of the only One who is able to protect you, preserve your life, and continue to unfold your destiny.

When a cyclone of trauma starts to bully your psyche and a twister of rejection begins to menace your emotional safety, in that moment, take a deep breath and hold on to these words from the sacred pages of Scripture:

There will be a shelter to give shade from the heat by day, and refuge and protection from the storm and the rain. —Isaiah 4:6

It is impossible to eliminate storms from one's life, but it is possible to run for Shelter and find that place of sweet but powerful protection. A storm-tossed disciple can abide in this peaceful refuge until the whirlwind passes by.

He who dwells in the shelter of the Most High will abide in the shadow of the Almighty. —Psalm 91:1

I shared the following quote with you earlier in this book, but let me remind you once again of something the great theologian Charles H. Spurgeon said:

I have learned to kiss the wave that throws me against the Rock of Ages.

It is amply clear that storms are an inevitable part of our lives this side of heaven's shores; in fact, none of us is immune to a Category 5 hurricane as we try to carve out an abundant life while living in our earthly bodies. However, we now know that going through a storm can be a fortifying experience as we discover how to throw off panic and determinedly choose to prevail. It is in the most volatile moments of a storm that a disciple of Jesus determines whether they are going to be filled with fear or with faith. No one else can make that choice for us.

When a storm is brewing on the horizon of your life, rather than post your pain on social media and complain about your lack of resources, focus on the only One who is able to protect, defend, and preserve you. Take time to pray, read the Word, and worship.

Sing for Joy!

But let all who take refuge in You be glad, let them ever sing for joy; and may You shelter them, that those who love Your name may exult in You. —Psalm 5:11

I have learned that "singing in the rain" is an especially effective response to a downpour of disappointing events. Never forget that when you worship the Lord in the middle of a monsoon, a shelter is created that, although it cannot be seen by the natural eye, provides a lovely place of warmth and protection.

As you wait in the impenetrable shelter of God's presence, and as you long for the storm to pass by, you will discover within you an uncommon strength that has never before been part of your inner being. You will be sustained, empowered, and propelled into God's purposes. His shelter is not just a hiding place from storms. If that were all it was, it would be enough—it would be more than enough. But I can assure you that the protection of God's presence is a place where an inner work is accomplished in our lives. In the middle of the storm, we become more like Him, and we inherit spiritual riches we had never before known were available to us. We are changed into people of valor and destiny. Even while the storm outside is wreaking havoc and unleashing destruction, within the storm shelter, we are protected and provided with a glorious sustenance. The storm has now become our finest hour as God's work is completed in our lives.

"It's time to thank God for the lessons the storm has taught you."

—Author unknown

Scriptures to Declare Before, During, and After the Storm

Then they cried to the LORD in their trouble, and He brought them out of their distresses. He caused the storm to be still, so that the waves of the sea were hushed. Then they were glad because they were quiet, so He guided them to their desired haven. Let them give thanks to the LORD for His lovingkindness, and for His wonders to the sons of men! —Psalm 107:28–31

[Jesus] said to them, "Why are you afraid, you men of little faith?" Then He got up and rebuked the winds and the sea, and it became perfectly calm. —Matthew 8:26

I said, "Oh, that I had wings like a dove! I would fly away and be at rest. Behold, I would wander far away, I would lodge in the wilderness. I would hasten to my place of refuge from the stormy wind and tempest." —Psalm 55:6–8

*The L*ORD *is good, a stronghold in the day of trouble, and He knows those who take refuge in Him.* —Nahum 1:7

*The L*ORD *is my light and my salvation; whom shall I fear? The L*ORD *is the defense of my life; whom shall I dread? When evildoers came upon me to devour my flesh, my adversaries and my enemies, they stumbled and fell. Though a host encamp against me, my heart will not fear; though war arise against me, in spite of this I shall be confident.* —Psalm 27:1–3

For You have been a defense for the helpless, a defense for the needy in his distress, a refuge from the storm, a shade from the heat. —Isaiah 25:4

But we have this treasure in earthen vessels, so that the surpassing greatness of the power will be of God and not from ourselves; we are afflicted in every way, but not crushed; perplexed, but not despairing; persecuted, but not forsaken; struck down, but not destroyed; always carrying about in the body the dying of Jesus, so that the life of Jesus also may be manifested in our body.

—2 Corinthians 4:7–10

The heavens will praise Your wonders, O LORD; Your faithfulness also in the assembly of the holy ones. For who in the skies is comparable to the LORD? Who among the sons of the mighty is like the LORD, a God greatly feared in the council of the holy ones, and awesome above all those who are around Him? O LORD God of hosts, who is like You, O mighty LORD? Your faithfulness also surrounds You. You rule the swelling of the sea; when its waves rise, You still them.

—Psalm 89:5–9

Do not fear, for I have redeemed you; I have called you by name; you are Mine! When you pass through the waters, I will be with you; and through the rivers, they will not overflow you. When you walk through the fire, you will not be scorched, nor will the flame burn you. For I am the LORD your God, the Holy One of Israel, your Savior.... Since you are precious in My sight, since you are honored and I love you, I will give other men in your place and other peoples in exchange for your life. Do not fear, for I am with you.

—Isaiah 43:1–5

Consider it all joy, my brethren, when you encounter various trials, knowing that the testing of your faith produces endurance. And let endurance have its perfect result, so that you may be perfect and complete, lacking in nothing. But if any of you lacks wisdom, let him ask of God, who gives to all generously and without reproach, and it will be given to him. But he must ask in faith without any doubting, for the one who doubts is like the surf of the sea, driven and tossed by the wind. —James 1:2–6

When I am afraid, I will put my trust in You. In God, whose word I praise, in God I have put my trust; I shall not be afraid. —Psalm 56:3–4

The steadfast of mind You will keep in perfect peace, because he trusts in You. Trust in the LORD forever, for in GOD the LORD, we have an everlasting Rock. —Isaiah 26:3–4

There will be a shelter to give shade from the heat by day, and refuge and protection from the storm and the rain. —Isaiah 4:6

---

*One thing I have asked from the LORD, that I shall seek: that I
may dwell in the house of the LORD all the days of my life, to behold
the beauty of the LORD and to meditate in His temple. For in the
day of trouble He will conceal me in His tabernacle; in the secret
place of His tent He will hide me; He will lift me up on a rock.
And now my head will be lifted up above my enemies around me,
and I will offer in His tent sacrifices with shouts of joy; I will sing,
yes, I will sing praises to the LORD.*   —Psalm 27:4–6

*He who dwells in the shelter of the Most High will abide in the
shadow of the Almighty. I will say to the LORD, "My refuge and
my fortress, my God, in whom I trust!" For it is He who delivers
you from the snare of the trapper and from the deadly pestilence.
He will cover you with His pinions, and under His wings you may
seek refuge; His faithfulness is a shield and bulwark. You will not
be afraid of the terror by night, or of the arrow that flies by day;
of the pestilence that stalks in darkness, or of the destruction that
lays waste at noon. A thousand may fall at your side and ten thousand at your right hand, but it shall not approach you. You will
only look on with your eyes and see the recompense of the wicked.
For you have made the LORD, my refuge, even the Most High,
your dwelling place. No evil will befall you, nor will any plague
come near your tent. For He will give His angels charge concerning you, to guard you in all your ways. They will bear you up in
their hands, that you do not strike your foot against a stone. You
will tread upon the lion and cobra, the young lion and the serpent
you will trample down. "Because he has loved Me, therefore I will
deliver him; I will set him securely on high, because he has known*

My name. He will call upon Me, and I will answer him; I will be with him in trouble; I will rescue him and honor him. With a long life I will satisfy him and let him see My salvation."

—Psalm 91:1–16

About the Author

Carol McLeod is a popular speaker at women's conferences and retreats through Carol McLeod Ministries. She is the author of ten books, including *Guide Your Mind, Guard Your Heart, Grace Your Tongue* (Whitaker House, 2018), *Joy for All Seasons* (Bridge-Logos, 2016), *Holy Estrogen* (Harrison House, 2012), and *Defiant Joy* (Thomas Nelson, 2006). Carol hosts a daily podcast, *A Jolt of Joy!* on the Charisma Podcast Network, and a weekly podcast, *The Joy of Motherhood*, which is listened to by thousands of moms around the world. Her blog, *Joy for the Journey* (formerly *A Cup of Tea with Carol*), has been named in the Top 50 Faith Blogs for Women. After her 2013 devotional *21 Days to Beat Depression* had nearly 100,000 downloads in the first month, YouVersion picked it up, where it has been read over 500,000 times in five years. She also has ten other devotionals on YouVersion, including *Guide Your Mind, Guard Your Heart, Grace Your Tongue*. Carol writes a weekly column for *Ministry Today* and often writes for *Charisma* magazine. She is also a frequent guest on and has cohosted *100 Huntley Street*. Her teaching DVD *The Rooms of a Woman's Heart* won a Telly Award in 2005 for excellence in religious programming. The first Women's Chaplain at Oral Roberts University, she currently serves on the university's Alumni Board of Directors.

Carol has been married to her college sweetheart, Craig, for nearly forty years and is the mother of five children in heaven and five children on earth. Carol and Craig are now enjoying their new titles as "Marmee and Pa" to seven captivating grandchildren! She and her husband have recently moved to Oklahoma, where Craig serves as the North American Director for Global Partners, a missions organization that plants churches in remote areas of the world.